DR. R.A. VERNON'S

10 RULES
OF DATING

Victory Media & Publishing Company
16781 Chagrin Boulevard #132
Shaker Heights, OH 44120
www.victorymp.com

DEDICATION

I dedicate this book to my daughter Cha'nae. You promised me when you were a little girl that you would keep yourself pure until marriage and so far you've made it through high school and college and you've kept your word. I can't wait to see you in all white at your wedding. Daddy loves you so much!

To my namesake Rainnell III, you're a teenager now and who says a man can't be a virgin when he gets married? No woman deserves to touch you until she marries you. Your name is R. A. Vernon and you're a king, don't ever forget that, my son!

I also dedicate this book to my niece, Altese. You have made it to your senior year untouched by any man. You are beautiful inside and out and Uncle Rainnell loves you so much.

Also, to my baby daughter, Little Victory who's only one year old at the time I'm writing this. I prophetically speak that no man will touch you until your honeymoon night. Let's read this part together and shout the night before your wedding!

To my cousin, Wendy, who has never let dating interrupt your destiny. You were the first person in our family to graduate from college with your bachelor's degree and now you have your master's degree. You inspired me all the way to my doctorate and God's going to give you a great husband.

Lastly, to the singles of "THE WORD" CHURCH, both male and

female, I know it's challenging at times to be grown and alone, most of you have made mistakes and a lot of you are even single parents, yet you keep coming each week asking God to make you more like Him. Pastor loves you guys and though I'm married, I'll try to keep being sensitive to the needs and struggles of singles in my messages.

PREFACE

A few summers ago, I taught a relationship series titled, "I Can't Get No Satisfaction." The big point of the series was that you can't depend on any human relationship to "satisfy" you completely, and that ultimately only a real abiding relationship with Jesus can do that.

Whenever I teach on relationships, the church is far more crowded than usual and that particular summer was no different. Both our weekend and Wednesday services were pretty much full. During the series, I decided to take one of the Wednesday messages and dedicate it to singles. I had been teaching heavily on marriage for a few weeks and I figured Wednesday would be a great time to speak to singles who were either dating or looking to date. The weather was beautiful, and in Cleveland, we really only get two weeks of summer and then it seems as though everyone hibernates for the winter. That said, the summertime, along with the holiday season, can both be very challenging times for people who are grown and alone. That particular Wednesday, I thought I would do a fun but necessary message on dating. Like most pastors will tell you, normally we get the idea before we get the title. I knew I wanted to talk about dating, but I wasn't sure what I would name the message. Then it hit me. I would title the message, "The R.A. Vernon Ten Rules of Dating." I prayed and asked God to give me the ten most important rules singles should know about dating. I got up that night and spent over an hour going from rule one to rule ten.

By the time I was done preaching the message, people in the congregation were already texting people saying, "You have to get tonight's message!" The line to purchase the message was one of the longest I've ever seen in our church, especially on a Wednesday, and by the next day, it was the talk of the city. Since then, thousands of people from all over the world have purchased that message and the series from which it came. Hundreds of pastors have taught it to their singles and saw their churches grow because of it. Honestly, I had no idea how desperate singles were for some practical instruction on dating. To this day, "The R.A. Vernon Ten Rules of Dating" is one of the most requested messages I've ever preached.

In all my years of teaching and preaching, I had never included my name in a title of a message, and you might be wondering why this one was the exception. Well, the reality is, the Bible says little to nothing about dating. In Hebrew culture, which is the dominant culture of the Bible, marriages were arranged. Your parents got together with my parents and decided we would get married. It had nothing to do with attraction, commonality, likes and dislikes or anything else. If our parents decided we would be married that was it. Now before you say that arranging marriages was crazy, look at the divorce rate now vis-à-vis during that time. I'm not suggesting that your parents pick your spouse, but if you have solid parents that you trust, why not ask their opinion about the person you are contemplating spending your life with? My adult kids won't date anybody I don't like. Not because I demand they don't, but because they honor my experience, discernment, and wisdom. Their mother and I have loved, honored, and respected each other in front of them, and both my son and daughter told me that they want what their mom and I have when they get married and they won't settle for less.

In this postmodern society in which we live, most people reading this are probably not as fortunate as my children. You didn't grow up watching a marriage you really respected and wanted to model. Coupled with that, the Bible says basically nothing about how to date, who you should date, when you should date, or what to do while dating.

Now the reality is, people are going to date and you can forget about us going back to the time of arranged marriages; that's not going to happen! So the situation we find ourselves in is this: there is no real biblical teaching on how to date, and marriages are no longer arranged, so that leaves Christian singles with no reference point or real resources as to how to do it. Consequently, most singles have been through the pain of a lot of relationships gone bad, especially women who just by their very nature give unreservedly when they love someone.

Now I know there are hundreds of secular books on dating, and most every popular magazine does some article a couple times a year on what to look for in a potential spouse. I would argue that most of that literature has little to none of God's perspective and heart concerning relationships. The reason why I titled this book *Dr. R.A. Vernon's 10 Rules of Dating,* is because in all honesty, these rules don't come directly from the Bible, though each rule has a biblical underpinning; nor do they come from any other source. They are the rules I feel the spirit of God gave me to help singles navigate through the often turbulent waters of dating. After 25 years of reading the Bible, being single and saved until I was 27, pastoring, and giving advice and guidance to thousands of singles at our church over the years, I think I have a pretty good grasp on the 10 rules you should follow before you say "I do!"

THREE TYPES OF SINGLES

Through my research and counsel over the years, I have discovered that there are basically **three kinds of singles. SINGLE AND SATISFIED, SINGLE AND SINNING, and SINGLE AND SEEKING.**

Single and Satisfied - These are people who for whatever reason, are content being single. They honestly and sincerely don't want to be with anyone right now. In some cases, these are individuals that have been through a lot with the opposite sex and just feel like they **can do bad all by themselves!** Some have been divorced, and others have been in one or more rough relationships that damaged them emotionally, financially, and sometimes even physically in a such a way that they have given up on dating altogether. In some rare cases, there are those who feel they have been called to a life of celibacy (such as priests or nuns), and are content serving Christ without ever getting married, or having sex.

One of the questions I ask singles who have given up on dating because of bad past relationships is this: Because you went to a couple of bad restaurants in your life, did you give up on eating? Of course not! You just found a better one that provided what you needed. I pray that you would get a copy of this book for some wounded single you know that has given up on love (because of previous drama) and God's ability to bless them with someone that would value them.

There is a major difference between SINGLE AND SATISFIED AND SINGLE AND SOILED! Some of you reading this think you're satisfied when really you're just scared—scared to trust again, scared of being hurt again, scared to believe again, and single parents are definitely scared for their kids to be abandoned again. The Bible is clear in 2 Timothy 1:7 (NLT) that "God has not given us a spirit of fear and timidity, but of power, love, and self-discipline." It's the enemy that wants you to feel your dating life is over and you should give up wanting or desiring to be loved in a romantic way. I've seen a lot of singles who claimed they were satisfied until the right person came along.

There is absolutely nothing wrong with being single and satisfied. As a matter-of-fact, the Bible highly recommends it. Paul the Apostle was single and satisfied. Read what he says regarding staying single (if possible).

1 Corinthians 7:8-9 (Message Bible): I do, though, tell the unmarried and widows that singleness might well be the best thing for them, as it has been for me. But if they can't manage their desires and emotions, they should by all means go ahead and get married. The difficulties of marriage are preferable by far to a sexually tortured life as a single.

He continues in verses 32-35.

1 Corinthians 7:32-35 (NLT): [32] I want you to be free from the concerns of this life. An unmarried man can spend his time doing the Lord's work and thinking how to please him. [33] But a married man has to think about his earthly responsibilities and how to please his wife.[34] His interests are divided. In the same way, a woman who is no longer married or has never been married can be devoted to the Lord and holy in body and in spirit. But a married woman has to think about her earthly responsibilities and how to please her husband. [35] I am saying this for your benefit, not to place restrictions on you. I want you to do whatever will help you serve the Lord best, with as few distractions as possible.

I think you get the point that Paul's desire to please God far outweighed his desire to be married. The reality is, most of us don't have the discipline or the God-given gift of celibacy. In such cases, Paul clearly recommends marriage.

There are many of you, who, like Paul, are so busy for God that you've decided that marriage is not for you. You are perfectly content to spend the rest of your life serving and pleasing Christ without what the New Living Translation of the Bible calls "distractions." Dating and marriage are without question distractions, but they are what I call "delightful distractions."

Falling in love and getting married require a lot of time

and energy—time and energy that you would otherwise give to God. That's just real. Paul, who at that time thought Jesus was coming right back, felt that dating and marriage were a waste of precious time. He felt that time could be used trying to get the whole world saved from hell. Of course 20 centuries later we know that Jesus didn't come back as soon as Paul thought he would.

If you're busy doing ministry, making money, pursuing education, and just feel that right now God has you working on you, then here is a great way to describe your current status: **SATISFIED FOR A SEASON**. In other words, in this "season" of your singleness it's not time to date. Maybe you're just coming out of a marriage or relationship, or you may have children who need you to tunnel focus on them right now. Maybe you are extremely busy at your church doing ministry and just know that right now is not the time for you to be with anyone. In that case, you are SATISFIED in this season and that's fine.

Many of you may be widows or widowers and have decided to follow Paul's advice and spend the rest of your days alone serving God. In addition, you may have loved your deceased spouse so much you just can't imagine starting over again with someone else. I often think about Coretta Scott King, who was still a very young, attractive woman, when Dr. King was killed. Have you ever asked yourself why a woman that young and beautiful stayed single the rest of her life? I'm sure brothers were coming at her left and right saying stupid stuff such as, "Hey girl, what's yo' name?" When some man would approach her, can you just imagine her thinking about her late husband who finished high school and went to Morehouse College at 15 years old, earned a Ph.D. from Boston University before he was 30, led the Montgomery bus boycott in 1955, led a march on Washington in 1963, won the Nobel Peace Prize in 1964, spearheaded the Voting Bill Act in 1965, and more than once was on the cover of Time Magazine? I can hear her asking any man who flirted with her one question, "Do you have a dream?"

Still other singles might simply have Paul's gift and desire to stay single. They're not gay, they're not on the down-low; they really have the ability to be happily grown and alone. They're probably not reading this because why would anybody truly satisfied want to read a book about dating?

Single and Sinning - Most singles are sexually active in some form. The reality is very few singles are celibate. Most of you reading this are Christian singles and sadly the majority of you are having sex. Make no mistake about it, I'm a Christian and a pastor; I believe the Bible, and the Bible clearly states sex out of wedlock is a sin and strongly speaks against it.

Ephesians 5:3 (NLT) "Let there be no sexual immorality, impurity, or greed among you. Such sins have no place among God's people."

1 Thessalonians 4:3 (NLT) "God's will is for you to be holy, so stay away from all sexual sin."

Notice the Bible says, "all sexual sin," which includes sex with yourself! To put it plainly, the only time sex is right is when it's between two married people. Period! All other sexual activity is viewed by God as sin. No matter what society says or how old fashioned it sounds, the Bible is still true. If you are watching pornography, masturbating, having phone sex with someone, sleeping with anyone or anything (including animals), it is all sinful and can and will hurt you in the long run.

If you are in the Single and Sinning category, in essence, you have no fear of God right now, or at least not enough to make you stop. Marriage is not on your mind; you have someone that meets your sexual needs or you satisfy yourself in some form. Many of you are believers, which is of course even worse, but whether you are in church or not, if you are involved in any form of sexual activity outside of marriage with no plan to stop, like it or not, right now you are SINGLE AND SINNING. In this book we will discuss in detail the damaging effects of sexual activity before marriage and challenge you toward a life of freedom through celibacy or a godly marriage.

Single and Seeking - If you bought this book, chances are you fit in this category. You want to give and receive love from someone, hopefully of the opposite sex. Seeking does not mean you are desperate. It does not mean you are pressed to be with someone; it simply means you are honest about who and how God made you. You are just not the single type. You want to be married. You want to make love to someone, maybe have children with them, serve God together, and all that goes with having a family. In that case, you are officially seeking.

Now one common myth I would like to debunk is that only men can seek. Most Christians base this assumption on Proverbs 18:22 where it says: "He who finds a wife finds a good thing and obtains favor from the Lord."

It's because of that one verse that the church has taught for years that a man should flirt with a woman and not the other way around. Let me state for the record that I agree 100 percent with that because I'm from the old school. But if seminary teaches you anything it is not to make the Bible fit your opinion. I personally believe that men like the idea of a chase. We're competitive and we like a good challenge. When a man asks you for your number and you say "No!" It keeps him up all night trying to figure out how to get you. When you won't kiss him or touch him, he'll probably propose in less than six months! That said though, that's simply my opinion; it's not biblical. The Bible does not say that a woman cannot approach a man. It is not a sin and it is not wrong for a female to walk up to a man and ask him out! Many couples met that way and have lived happily ever after. However, when a woman approaches a man, he assumes that since she was the aggressor she will be easy to sleep with, which does not have to be the case. Again, I would rather the man be the aggressor but let God lead you, my sister.

Whether you are male or female, if you are SINGLE AND SEEKING this book is going to give you ten rules you should follow before you say, "I do" to anyone. To those of you who may have heard me teach the original message, since then I've prayerfully changed a couple of the original rules. I've thought long and hard about these 10 things and I pray that as you read them you will take each one serious and not compromise on any of them. The biggest choice you will ever make in your life other than choosing Christ as your Savior will be who you say "I do" to. Currently, over 50 percent of marriages end in divorce and that includes Christian marriages. I'm convinced that had those couples had a dating resource to guide them in their choices that number would be lower. Read each rule, don't compromise on any of them, and most of all pray, pray, pray, before you make the second biggest choice of your life.

RULE 1

THERE MUST BE PHYSICAL ATTRACTION

To all the Christians who are reading this book, please don't consider me a heretic because the first rule isn't "They must love Jesus" (By the way, that is rule number 2). The fact is, I've counseled enough struggling married couples to know how important physical attraction is, especially to most men. This is one of the few rules that is kind of gender specific.

We cannot escape the reality that some things tend to be more important to men than women and vice versa. My research concludes that the first thing that draws you to someone is how good they look to you, not how spiritual they are. If the average single man, Christian or not, is walking down the street, he does not look at a woman and say "Man! Look at the Holy Spirit on her!" The first thing he normally notices is her figure and her face. If he's not physically attracted to her, then he's probably not going to approach her to find out if she is a believer, unless of course, he's just out evangelizing.

Years ago, when I first started developing these ten rules, I knew it was critical for me to begin with physical attraction. I can't tell you how many couples I've had to help work through intimacy issues over the years because the husband was not attracted to his wife. Get this now: he actually married a woman who did not have the physical attributes he found desirable, and wondered why they were struggling in the bedroom. I have had men actually say to me, "I like a woman with big breasts and a big behind," when his wife had neither. How crazy is that? He could have prayerfully waited for a woman who possessed what he liked and needed physically to be turned on continually by her.

As a married man, I can tell you that marriage is going to keep you on your knees, but one prayer you should never have to pray is "Lord, please make my wife's breasts and behind get bigger." A woman should never pray, "Lord, please make my husband taller and darker." Marry the person who has attributes that you like. While it may sound superficial or unspiritual to some, let me suggest to you that it's biblical. Beauty and attraction, especially for men throughout the scripture, are very important factors.   ·

Genesis 12:11 (NLT) As he was approaching the border of Egypt, Abram said to his wife, Sarai, "Look, you are a very beautiful woman."

Genesis 26:7 (NLT) When the men of the place asked about his wife, he said, "She is my sister," for he was afraid to say, "my wife," thinking, " the men of the place might kill me on account of Rebekah, for she is beautiful."

Both Abram and his son Isaac referred to their own wives as beautiful. Notice I said their "own wives" because beauty is truly in the eye of the beholder. The only opinion that matters when it comes to whether someone who you're interested in is physically attractive is yours. I know men who are only attracted to heavier women. I know other brothers who only like slender women. Some women love dark men, others lighter-skinned men. The big point is this: get what you like and don't compromise.

Date someone with the figure and the face that you need to be satisfied physically. Here is a great scripture regarding both the former and the latter:

Genesis 29:16-18 (NLT) Now Laban had two daughters. The older daughter was named Leah, and the younger one was Rachel. [17] There was no sparkle in Leah's eyes, but Rachel had a beautiful figure and a lovely face. [18] Since Jacob was in love with Rachel, he told her father, "I'll work for you for seven years if you'll give me Rachel, your younger daughter, as my wife."

I love the New Living Translation. It says, "Rachel had a beautiful figure and a lovely face." No man reading this should date anyone who does not have the "beautiful figure and lovely face" that he desires. To every woman reading this who does not see herself as beautiful and well-built, know that God has a brother who will be floored when he meets you. Don't settle for any man who isn't smitten by your very presence.

BE YOUR BEST SELF

This book is too important to singles for me not to be blatantly honest. It is highly essential that a single woman with the desire to be married look as good as she can. I'm not talking about how tall, short, light or dark you are; that is totally out of your control. I'm talking about being as physically fit and healthy as you can be. Avoid allowing your weight to escalate because of bad eating habits or lack of exercise. Every woman is different and will not be the same size, color, or height, so if you're a woman reading this, don't fret over the unchangeable attributes of your physical appearance. Just be your best self! Keep your hair and nails done. If you can't afford to have them done, do them yourself to the best of your ability. Dress as nice and as feminine as you can without being provocative (Never compromise your Christianity to be cute). As I said earlier, men are turned on by sight. That's the way God made us!

WOMEN AND MEN ARE JUST DIFFERENT

Two of the best books I've ever read on the differences between men and women are *Men are from Mars, Women from Venus* by John Gray and *His Needs Her Needs* by Willard Harley. (I highly recommend all singles read both before marriage). Understanding the fact that men and women were created by God with different needs and desires is paramount to having any successful relationship. Equally important is having an adequate understanding of how men and women are different.

Most single women reading this book would love to have a great-looking, well-built man approach them. But if he's not the handsomest guy on the planet, is that a deal breaker? No! If he approaches you in a respectful manner and presents himself as a gentleman, the reality is, for most women, he does not have to be as good-looking as Will Smith to have a chance. If he's dressed nice, in a uniform that shows he's coming from a job of some sort, or donning a hard hat, flannel, and worn-out jeans indicating he's been making a living laying bricks all day, a woman still might find him attractive based on other things we'll address in our other nine rules.

Now before you say it, let me! I know there are women reading this who disagree with me because you consider physical attraction number one on your list of prerequisites for dating. At the same time, there are some men reading this thinking that there are things much more important to them than being physically attracted to a woman. I certainly respect and understand how you feel; however, in general, my research concludes that those who share this view are the exception and not the norm.

THERE IS AN ELEPHANT IN THE ROOM

Since the majority of singles reading this book are probably Christians, let me answer the question you know you want to ask: WHAT IF THEY ARE NOT GOOD IN BED?

Let me state emphatically that I believe that premarital sex is wrong because it is a sin. The Bible says in 1 Corinthians 6:18-20 (NLT): "Run from sexual sin! No other sin so clearly affects the body as this one does. For sexual immorality is a sin against your own body. [19] Don't you realize that your body is the temple of the Holy Spirit, who lives in you and was given to you by God? You do not belong to yourself, [20] for God bought you with a high price. So you must honor God with your body."

The Bible is clear that the only person you should make love to is your spouse and the only way to have sex biblically is within the sacred confines of marriage.

1 Corinthians 7:1-2 (NLT) - Now regarding the questions you asked in your letter. Yes, it is good to live a celibate life. [2] But because there is so much sexual immorality, each man should have his own wife, and each woman should have her own husband.

Most singles reading this book did not follow the advice of Paul on remaining celibate until marriage, and you've had one or more sexual partners. Consequently, your sexual past can lead to certain expectations and inevitable comparisons when it comes to the marriage bed.

All right, let me say it straight. When a single Christian meets someone whom they are attracted to (and hopefully by the end of this book you will know exactly what to look for and expect from any person you consider marrying), the one thing you don't know if you commit to celibacy (which, by the way, is Rule 10) is how you will click between the sheets. I'll discuss this at length when I cover Rule 10. But how will you know if you are sexually compatible with the person if you wait until honeymoon night to have sex? I'm glad you asked!

The answer is, BY FAITH! I'm not trying to over spiritualize this concern, but I really mean, BY FAITH! You should seek God's will concerning the person you are interested in to the point of knowing undoubtedly that He joined you together. Why would God adjoin you to someone who could not satisfy you sexually when He knows how important sex is in marriage?

PREVIOUS PARTNERS

Remember, it is God's will that you save yourself sexually for your spouse. Most people reading this book did not. This leads to married individuals making comparisons God never intended. Let's not play games. If a man has had more women and sexual experiences than he can count on one hand, saved or not, this is going to have some effect on his marriage. In fact, even if you've only been with one woman or man, past sexual encounters can compromise your ability to achieve sexual contentment or gratification in your future marital relationship, by subtly and subconsciously permeating your most intimate moments with images from your past. Your memories of the way another person used to perform during sex can seriously compromise you and your spouse's sexual confidence—yours in your spouse's ability to bring you the same kind of satisfaction you may have received from a previous partner, and your spouse may suffer insecurities if he or she senses they are not satisfying you sexually.

It is not God's will for your future spouse to be compared to anyone, which is why you must abandon any apprehension regarding a future spouse's sexual performance and rely instead on your faith in God's ability to give you exactly what you want in bed.

When you have made the mistake of having premarital sex, you must believe by faith, trust the blood of Jesus, and rely on the power of the Holy Spirit to not only remove those previous soul ties (the metaphysical adhesive that bonds you to another person when you have sexual intercourse with them), but also guide you to the person who is sexually compatible with you.

Given the fact that most of you reading this are not virgins, allow me to encourage you here. The fact that you have had premarital sex will not prevent you from achieving sexual affinity in marriage. God is sovereign, and His ability to remove toxic impressions from your memory that have the potential to infringe on a union that He sanctioned is unaffected by the breadth, depth, or length of your sexual history. In other words, the fact that you have a sexual past will not prevent you from having an enjoyable sex life in marriage, BUT, it can, if you continue opening yourself up to illegitimate sexual experiences. You cannot expect God to honor your marital choice if you don't honor Him during your single season. If you are not celibate now and you want to have a marriage characterized by purity, intimacy, and an unadulterated sexual connection, make the decision to abstain from any further sexual interaction. Believe me; you'll be glad you did.

The first rule of dating is that there must be physical attraction, but, it is not the most important rule. You'll discover, as I continue to delineate the other nine rules, there are other things that will be far more significant in the long haul than physical appearance.

If a man lacks the will to provide for himself and his family, a woman will hardly notice how fine he is. If a woman constantly emasculates and disrespects her man with harsh words and derisive looks, it will be difficult for him to even remember the beauty he once saw in her.

But, being physically attracted to a person you are considering dating is rule number one. The first attraction is not spiritual, emotional, or even mental. How could I know any of the aforementioned things about a woman unless I first approached her and had a conversation with her? Why would I approach her if nothing about her physical appearance appeals to me? As shallow as this may sound to some, it's nonetheless true.

For a woman, if a guy whom she has never seen before approaches her with questionable breath, dirty clothes, and a disheveled and unkempt appearance overall, chances are, if he does have a great heart, she'll never know it. What would make her want to hear anything he has to say if he looks like he doesn't care about his appearance? Physical attraction is not to be minimized.

Rule 1: There Must Be Physical Attraction
Critical Thinking Points

Take a few minutes to reflect on the contents of the chapter.
Write down your initial thoughts, reactions and feelings.
Based on the information you've read,
what are the most important take-away points.

I understand the point. I realized that I need to
be attractive(d) to me if anyone else is to be too.
It really hit me about the self pleasuring pad. I knew
it was a sin but didn't think it meant I was soiled.

I do have issues w/ believing that I am deserving of
love. More self-esteem issues on my part. I do
wonder if I'm called re celibacy bc I don't know
what I want in a partner. I've always just taken
whatever comes my way. No more. I know that right
now I'm no good for anyone.

My deal. No sex period.
Look good daily.
Be kind to me.

RULE 2

THEY MUST LOVE JESUS

It's no secret to most of you reading this that I am a pastor. One of my goals in writing this book was to write it in such a way that even people who don't frequently attend church would at least give the rules a shot. If you've been trying to date for years and have had no real success; if you're tired of trying to keep up with the games people play, tired of enduring the emptiness of premarital sex and all the residual consequences that come with it; it is my prayer that I can help you with all these concerns by offering solid advice that you can put into practice immediately.

But my first and foremost goal is to get you to fall in love with Jesus Christ. He is ultimately the only One who can and will fill the void that so often singles try to fill with a person, or in some cases, persons. I am not suggesting that you should not desire the love of another; however, the love that Jesus Christ can give you greatly surpasses the capacity that any earthly being has to love you. Secondly, I hope that by the end of this book, you understand the importance of loving Him and make knowing Him a prerequisite for anyone you date.

Thus, Rule 2 is: They must love Jesus.

Notice I didn't say, "They must go to church." The devil goes to church and unlike many Christians, he gets there on time and never misses. Just in case you don't finish the other eight rules in this lifetime, make sure you at least finish this chapter.

Don't date anyone who does not love Jesus more than they love you. I can't tell you all the horror stories my wife and I have heard over the years from people in our church that made the choice to marry an unbeliever and were dealing with the regrettable consequences of living with someone day after day who had no fear and reverence for God.

It's my story and I'm sticking to it—the first rule of dating is that there must be physical attraction, but the very next question you should want answered after asking the person's name is whether or not they know Jesus—intimately. Not, "What's your sign?" (Please don't get me started on that "sign" stuff; I want to keep this book simple and easy to read).

Be careful of even those who have met Jesus, believe in Him, and claim to know Him, but do not appear to have a relationship with Him. There will be certain situations where this is glaringly obvious, and others, well...not so much.

For example, you're at the gym getting ready for your morning workout, and while walking by the basketball court, you observe a guy who walks like Idris, has a body like Beckham, and the athleticism of LeBron. He notices you looking at him, and since he's just shooting around, decides to pass the basketball to a buddy and jog on over to you.

As he gets closer, you realize he has all the facial features you like—goatee, strong jaw line, straight teeth, and is even sporting a nice chain, dangling a diamond Jesus hanging on a platinum cross. You can't help but smile at the sheer thought of someone this fine and saved (He has to be, right? After all, he's wearing Jesus around his neck!) making his way over to you to strike up a conversation that just might lead to something more.

"Hi. I'm Matthew," he says. "You are?"

Smitten, is what you want to say, but you manage to say instead, "Tina."

"Well, Tina, it's nice to meet you. Can't really talk long, 'cause I'm warming up for a *bleeping* game, but I was wondering if I could get your number and *bleep*, maybe hook up for a few drinks later."

Your heart sinks, and we all know why. Uh, this guy, while he has everything you want physically, is probably not going to have anything you need spiritually. At this point, it's really time to politely walk away, but let's go ahead and assess the situation for the heck of it.

WARNING SIGN #1:

Matthew's language is not reflective of someone who represents Christ. In addition, call me old-fashioned, but a brother who approaches a woman and uses profanity in his pickup line is not worth further conversations. He doesn't respect you. (Now this may be problematic if you're a woman who uses more curse words than a voodoo doctor, but I'll take for granted this isn't the case).

WARNING SIGN #2:

Matthew suggests going out for drinks later, and Tina knows he's not talking about sparkling water. Chances are, if he has a strong relationship with Christ, he understands the implications of drinking, what even "casual" alcohol consumption can lead to, and that social drinking, especially as a method of courtship is a behavior atypical of a Christian man whose focus is on trying to build and maintain his relationship with Christ. He also understands that even if he's not drinking to get drunk, the chances of him being seen drinking in a public, secular setting puts both his integrity and ministry at risk. If he cared about his character, he would not be willing to so carelessly sacrifice it.

WARNING SIGN #3:

Matthew, though wearing a chain that represents the crucifixion of Christ, is clearly just being fashionable. Nothing in his choice of words or his suggestions is reflective of a person who understands the symbolic significance of Christ's death on the cross, not to mention the hypocrisy and insolence of toting Jesus around, flaunting Him in a manner contradictory to the lifestyle He came to Earth to represent.

Now to be fair to Matthew, we're not going to deem him unsaved. He very well might be. What should be pretty clear though, is his lack of spiritual maturity; hence, he might have met Christ, but based on his presentation, the likelihood of him really knowing Him in a personal manner is very low.

Again, after only that brief exchange, if what Tina is looking for is a godly man with principles and a genuine love and reverence for Christ, then she needs to put her earbuds in (to make it clear the conversation is over), say "No, thank you," and trot away from him and over to the treadmill just as smoothly as Matthew jogged toward her from the court. Ladies, this is not the type of guy that you want to entertain.

In another situation, the signs denoting whether or not a person's spiritual walk is up to par may not be as evident. Her conversation may be completely respectful and she may even mention God or church in her initial dialogue with you. It may take a few more conversations, closely observing her choice of words (what she says and what she doesn't say), and a thorough scrutiny of her behavior to analyze whether or not she is truly at the level in her Christian walk you need her to be.

Do the work to discover their spiritual altitude. I mean if you really think about it, does it matter what else we have in common if we don't have the commonality of Christianity? Life is a trip at times when you're by yourself, even with Jesus. How in the heck are we going to survive it without Him, especially when you add another person's personality, issues, concerns, needs, desires, habits, flaws, and sinful nature to your own? We may not have everything in common and that's fine, but without question, we have to agree on Jesus, and we need to be on a similar spiritual plane.

Amos 3:3 (NLT) - Can two people walk together without agreeing on the direction?

It may be difficult to demand that someone pour into you spiritually everyday if you are unwilling or unable to do the same for them. I don't know if it's fair to require a mate to pray for you on a regular basis, when it's been so long since you and God talked that you feel awkward whenever you're asked to pray. Lack of spiritual knowledge on one mate's behalf may truly make them incompatible with you if you're a person who considers Bible reading an important part of your daily regimen. A person's spiritual incompetence can be extremely frustrating in times when you need insight, or when you want to have a conversation about the most important relationship in your life—your relationship with Jesus Christ.

By the same token, if you're comfortable where you are spiritually and don't see the need to deepen your relationship with Christ any further, then you probably are not going to be happy with the person who wants to talk about how good God is all the time. You may become annoyed if the person asks you to pray with them, study the Bible together, or seek God for deeper revelation about a particular situation they're going through, if you consider spending time with God to be something only to be done on Sundays or Wednesdays. Or perhaps you do feel you should be spending more time with God, but at this time, your conviction about the latter is not strong enough to inspire you to change. If a person tries to encourage that change before you are ready, you'll only end up frustrated and possibly even resentful that he or she is trying to change you.

The point is, when you're choosing a mate, the person should have analogous goals when it comes to spirituality (and other areas as well—but we'll discuss that in the next chapter) and you should have a mutual understanding regarding each other's spiritual state to avoid feelings of dissatisfaction surfacing later. I am not contending that two people with varying levels of spirituality cannot have a meaningful relationship. It is possible to be content with someone who is more or less spiritual than you, as long as you realize what implications this can and will have on your relationship. Your future mate may not be the person you have deep theological discussions with; however, he or she may be able to listen to you talk about it for hours, intrigued by your passion for God, and that may be all you need. They may not be capable of engaging you in stimulating discourse on the topic, but if you're clear on what their limitations are ahead of time, their inability to offer you a well-thought-out response when you bring up the interpretive dilemma of the doctrine of theism won't prove problematic.

Conversely, if you're not exactly a biblical scholar but you desire to learn more about Christ, then a person with a higher spiritual education than you may be quite attractive. A connection like this one could be replete with opportunity for two individuals to build a loving, healthy, bond together defined by admiration, respect and a common understanding of what each other's strengths and weaknesses are.

However, please listen to me when I tell you that there is no woman sexy enough, no man rich enough, and no house big enough to take the place of an authentic relationship with Christ.

What happens if my little daughter gets fatally sick and I don't have a praying spouse? What happens if I get diagnosed with something deadly and I don't have a spouse who is at least familiar with God enough to feel comfortable interceding on my behalf? What happens if I am traveling on business and somebody better looking than me approaches my spouse and makes them an offer they don't have the POWER to refuse? That's right. I said, POWER! It takes knowing Jesus and being Spirit-filled to reject the enemy's schemes, and trust me; he is coming for your marriage!

1 Peter 5:8-9 (NLT) - Stay alert! Watch out for your great enemy, the devil. He prowls around like a roaring lion, looking for someone to devour. [9] Stand firm against him, and be strong in your faith.

Just as it is important that a person you are considering marrying be in love with Jesus, the same applies for you, which is why I mentioned being on a similar spiritual plane earlier. You too should be in love with Jesus. Knowing Him personally will give you an indispensable edge in dating and you want that advantage. There are so many people with their own goals in mind when they approach you, and many times, those goals won't even include starting a long-term, loving, holy relationship. Unfortunately, especially for women who want to love and be loved, it's not always easy to detect what a person's objectives are at the onset.

However, when you have a relationship with Christ, He'll talk to you, and without the impediment of persistent sin blocking your ability to hear clearly, you'll be able to discern the motives of those with impure intentions and make sensible decisions long before you've taken any emotional risks. Being in tune with the Holy Spirit can save you considerable time, effort, and energy, and eliminate the possibility of weeks, months, and even years laden with confusion, frustration, and disappointment.

Before you begin a relationship with anyone, I would strongly recommend taking inventory of your relationship with Christ, and evaluating where you are in your faith. Whatever that level is, that's the degree to which you are going to be successful in your relationship with a human being. The stronger your relationship with Christ, the better chances you have at selecting the mate He would have you to be with and the more likely you are to experience joy and satisfaction in a relationship that will ultimately lead to marriage. If your relationship with God is weak or shallow, you should have a commensurate expectation level for having a successful dating experience. I can't stress it enough; you need God's guidance in selecting a mate.

We'll touch on this more when we discuss rule 3, but spiritual compatibility, on any level, is critical in marriage. I can say with confidence that marriage is the most difficult relationship you will ever have to maintain. Being with one person forever is not natural; it is supernatural—a spiritual discipline that takes a lifetime to perfect. You better be pretty sure the person is worth it before you choose.

WHAT'S LOVE GOT TO DO WITH IT?

Notice Peter says, "Stand firm against him, and be strong in your faith." My question is, how can the person you're married to stand strong, when they have no faith? What's going to keep them from jumping on you, cheating on you, or cursing you out? I know you're thinking that the thing that should and would keep them from doing all the horrific stuff above would be the "love" that they have for you. The problem is if they are not believers, they don't possess the kind of love that only a relationship with Christ can foster.

Romans 5:3-5 (NLT) - We can rejoice, too, when we run into problems and trials, for we know that they help us develop endurance. [4] And endurance develops strength of character, and character strengthens our confident hope of salvation. [5] And this hope will not lead to disappointment. For we know how dearly God loves us, because he has given us the Holy Spirit to fill our hearts with his love.

The 'L' word is a trip! If you're reading this, chances are you've been in love before and it didn't work out, or, at some point in your life, you would like to love again. It's possible that you haven't ever experienced being in love, and you're looking to "fall" for the first time.

One of my favorite movies of all time (along with *The Godfather*, Parts 1 and 2—keep me lifted in prayer), is the Oscar-winning hit movie *Forrest Gump*. There is a great line in the movie where Jenny tries to convince Forrest that he does not really love her. Forrest then says to Jenny "I may not be a smart man but I know what love is." My question to all singles including divorcees, widows, and widowers is, "Did you and do you know what love is?"

In the Greek language the word love is much more loaded than it is in English. I'm going to give the simplest and quickest teaching on it I can.

The Six Types of Love

Mania –This obsessive, jealous love style is characterized by self-defeating emotions, desperate attempts to force affection from the beloved, and the inability to believe in or trust any affection the loved one actually does display. The manic lover is desperate to fall in love and to be loved, begins immediately to imagine a future with the partner, wants to see the partner daily, tries to force the partner to show love and commitment, distrusts the partner's sincerity, and is extremely possessive.[1] This is the love of possession. Mania encompasses the idea of obsessively desiring to own or control. It is generally seen as taking over the "lover" like insanity – thus the connection to modern concepts of madness (kleptomania, pyromania). It is like the opposite of a phobia – an obsessive need to avoid something. "Mania" is translated as "madness" and "beside yourself" in Acts 26.

Eros – Eros is the root word for "erotic," but it does not describe sexual love only; it actually describes all emotional love, or the feeling of being in love. Eros love is that insatiable desire to be near the object of desire. This is the exciting, passionate, nervous feeling that sweeps over people in appropriate circumstances.

This is the love that says "I love how you make me feel." As an emotion, eros changes, sometimes suddenly. Remember that it is entirely based on circumstances and on the target of its emotion. As an emotion alone, it is morally neutral; however, it can just as easily lead to lust (sinful desire) as it can passion. It is also a good picture to think of eros as the fruit and flowers of a new relationship. Eros is not a bad thing, but it is not necessarily a good thing either, as it is often this type love, unbridled, that leads to misguided decisions

1. Pamela C. Regan. The Mating Game: a Primer on Love, Sex, and Marriage. 2nd ed. Thousand Oaks: Sage, 2008.(126)

about intimacy with the opposite sex.

Philos love, or brotherly/friendship love - is the next kind we will look at. Philos describes the love between two people who have common interests and experiences, or a fondness for. Hemophiliacs apparently seemed to ancient doctors to have a "fondness" to bleeding, for example.

Unlike eros, which pulses up and down like waves on the ocean, philos steadily grows, like a building being constructed stone by stone. For this reason, when close friends are separated for a while and reunited, they will often say "it is like we picked up exactly where we left off." Philos is half about the circumstances, and half about the commitment of two people to one another; it says "I love who we are together," or in case of a non person: "I am fond of this food." Philos love generally grows over time except in the case of some kind of betrayal. It is commonly used in the New Testament, as in Matthew 10:37, John 12:25, and Revelation 3:19.

Storgy – We will not spend much time here; storgy is the love one has for a dependent. It is commonly called "motherly love." It is entirely based on the relationship between the "lover" and the "lovee." When the dependent is no longer dependent, this love remains only in its emotional remnants. It is one of the stronger loves, because it involves a commitment that relies on only one trait of the receiver – that he or she is dependent. This type of love is toxic to a marriage under normal circumstances. Marriages that look more like a mother/son or father/daughter relationship will quickly move downhill.

Agape – Agape love is the final of the six loves we look at here. Agape love is entirely about the lover, and has nothing whatsoever to do with the one loved. Agape love, in its purest form, requires no payment or favor in response. The most common word for God's love for us is agape (John 3:16) and the love we are commanded to have for one another (Matthew 5:44, 1 Corinthians 13). This lack of input from the recipient makes it possible for us to love our enemies even though we may not like them or the situation they have put us in, because agape love is not in any way dependent on circumstances. It says, "I love you because I choose/commit to." Unlike eros or philos, agape creates a straight line that neither fades nor grows in its perfect form, which of course only exists from God outward, though many people marry out of eros love alone. They make vows that speak of commitment despite any circumstance: richer/poorer, better/worse, sickness/health. This kind of love is about a commitment to the very best for another, no matter what emotions or feelings exist! You can see why in the King James Version of the Bible, agape was usually translated as "charity." It is a love freely given, and freely committed to. For a more in depth look at its aspects, look at 1 Corinthians 13.[2]

To those of you that feel like you're in love with someone, there are not many greater feelings in the world; savor it. However, there is no love like the love Jesus puts in the heart of a Spirit-filled believer, so please don't make the mistake of sacrificing that love for the others. Make sure whomever you date loves Jesus.

THIS COULD BE DANGEROUS

I must admit that I went back and forth on whether I should add this next part, but I think that I would be compromising the integrity of this book by omitting valuable albeit somewhat polemical information. If someone who is unsaved approaches you, it is possible for God to use you to evangelize to them. Their ultimate end may only be to get you, but what they don't know is once they

2. Chris Legg. "5 Greek Words for "Love"." Chris Legg, LPC. http://chrismlegg.com/2009/10/01/5-greek-words-for-love-agape/ (accessed October 16, 2011).

experience the love of Christ, their goal will be so much bigger than you.

It is important that when a non-Christian approaches you, you make it crystal clear that you don't date unbelievers. Sometimes, a lot of times, the conversation will end there. The reality is, Christians and non-Christians have different agendas, different objectives when it comes to lifestyle choices, and very little in common when it comes to life, period. This is not a condemnation of unbelievers, but rather an important distinction to emphasize exactly why believers and unbelievers don't and won't mesh well as a couple.

As Christians, we live for Christ. Our standard of living reflects the Word of God. We believe the Bible, the importance of honoring God in our daily walk, and that everything we do is to be done with purposeful diligence. When it comes to relationships, we don't date to have fun, to avoid loneliness, or to experience what it's like to be with different people. We consider dating an assignment—a mission with the objective of finding the one that God would be pleased to have us unite with. For an unbeliever, these things are probably not as important, and dissimilar spiritual values will cause division, pointless dissension, and distress almost immediately.

However, if the conversation doesn't end as soon as you tell them you don't date people outside of your faith and they express interest in wanting to know more about your beliefs, by all means, share the Gospel of Jesus Christ with them. Your divine commission as a witness for Christ is to evangelize to the unsaved. Dating is a secondary aim if the opportunity to get someone saved presents itself. You should even take it a step further and invite them to come to church with you.

But, let's keep it real. If you go to a church that you love for whatever reason, but you know the average first-time visitor won't enjoy the service, please take them to a church in your city that's relevant, contemporary, and teaching the truth of God's Word. The last thing you want to do is take them to your great-grandmother's church where the singing is dry and the preaching is boring. This just might be their first impression of the Christian worship service, or at least their first impression in a very long time. Don't be responsible for turning them off to Christ or for them receiving a poor perception of church because you simply wanted to bring someone to your home church.

Bear in mind, this is not a date; this is evangelism. He doesn't get to date you until he gets saved and the Spirit of God reveals to you that he is sincere about his new walk with Jesus. The reason why I had some trepidation about adding this is because people will often do whatever it takes to get you in bed, including joining your church! However, I suppose you don't really have to worry about being physical since rule number 10 will solve that.

Admittedly, I do have people in my church that hooked up with people who were not believers when they met, but the unbelieving person saw Christ in the person who was a believer, was won over to the Lord's side, and never looked back. I began this section the way I did, reluctantly disclosing this exception, because I do not believe this is a useful posture to have when dating. I don't think you should even give yourself the forged hope of believing that one day, because he appears to be a nice guy, he'll give his heart to the Lord, and to you too.

The reality is, if it happens, it's a twofold blessing to be sure. But, if your heart is set on the person being your soul mate from the beginning, you are setting yourself up for clouded judgment later on, when you'll need to be able to see objectively. Your motives, when bringing an unbeliever to the Lord, need to be grounded in your desire to see the person saved from a future of eternal damnation, not your desire to see the person in your future. If not, you'll believe what you want to believe so that you can get your needs met. Trust me. If he is not truly saved, you don't want him.

Determining their sincerity will take time. You can't prove how much you love Christ and how committed you are to the cause of Christianity in a month. I have had men in my church go through six months of new members classes, small groups, and any other prerequisite for getting involved in ministry, just to win the affection of a spiritually mature young woman in my church only to reveal later that he really only wanted her, not Christ. Of course by that time, if she wasn't vigilant and attentive in her observation of his motives and behavior, she fell for him, and was emotionally wrecked when she found out his faith was feigned.

PROVE SOMETHING

If a person claims to be a believer when you meet them, don't let profession be enough. Make them prove something! A good barometer for a person's spirituality is a solid juxtaposition of what they say to what they show. Bible readers know that Galatians 5: 22-23 lists what we call the Fruit of the Spirit. (I tell our church all the time that you can also call it the Proof of the Spirit).

Galatians 5:22-23 – [22] But the Holy Spirit produces this kind of fruit in our lives: love, joy, peace, patience, kindness, goodness, faithfulness, [23] gentleness, and self-control. There is no law against these things.

If you don't see these characteristics in a person, there is a good chance they don't have an authentic relationship with Jesus and are not Spirit-filled. I would really consider moving on quickly and not settling for less than God wants you to have.

Rule 2: They Must Love Jesus
Critical Thinking Points

RULE 3

THERE MUST BE COMPATIBILITY AND CONNECTIVITY

As important as it is to have Christ in common as a couple, it's not enough. If I consider a person to be a potential spouse, we have to be able to talk about more than the Bible. We have to be able to connect on several levels. Take it from someone who loves to hang out with his wife. We relate on everything from the bedroom to the bank account and yes, we both love the Lord with a passion, but trust me when I tell you, you need more than Jesus in common to have an enjoyable relationship.

So many people go out with each other for years, set a date, plan the wedding, get married, buy a home, and even have children together before they finally come to the dreadful reality that they have nothing in common. They love each other and are attracted to one another on one or more levels, or they probably would never have made it that far; however, being married to someone with whom you have very little in common can lead you straight into a miserable, regrettable, existence.

By no means am I suggesting that anybody can ever be everything you want or that you will have complete commonality in every area. There will be some things about whomever you choose to marry that will drive you nuts at times. That's why you have to make sure there is enough connection and compatibility to offset the things that will surely irritate you. Get to know the person's likes, dislikes, and idiosyncrasies. Ask all the questions you can think of. Remember, for you, dating is an assignment. You're trying to figure out as fast as you can if this person has the potential to be your spouse. Start your investigation immediately.

CAN WE TALK?

If you're a person who enjoys conversations rich with intellectual stimuli, philosophical repartee, and scholarly debates, then definitely engage your potential mate in this sort of discourse right away. See if the person has the willingness, and perhaps more important, the ability to talk about the things that are significant and rousing to you. You must ask yourself right away (no matter how physically attractive the person may be), "Can she excite me mentally for the rest of my life and if not, is that a deal breaker?" If it is, quickly end the relationship and wait for God's person to come along.

When we talk about connectivity and compatibility, it's important that this occurs on several levels, the first two being physical and spiritual. Regarding spirituality, as we discussed in the previous chapter, though being a Christian should be an absolute prerequisite for anyone you date, that alone may not be enough based on your level of spiritual maturity. God forbid something happens and my wife, Victory, goes to heaven before me (and I pray I go first). If something were to happen to her and I am still young enough and willing to remarry, it would take an extraordinary woman to help me pastor the thousands of people under my care. Being a Christian would not be enough. Her level of spirituality would have to well exceed that of the average Christian woman.

Number one, I've been saved and in ministry for over twenty-five years. Two, my assignment of pastoring a mega church requires someone who can pray me through all the challenges and pressures that come with what I do. I said all of that to say this: if you've been saved a long time like me and are really mature in the Lord, not only does the person need to be saved, they need to be spiritually seasoned enough to relate to you. Sometimes, in all humility, you just have to tell a brother, "You might be cute, but I don't have time to teach you John 3:16! I've walked with God too long and too deeply to hook up with someone who is just getting to know the Lord." That doesn't make you arrogant; that makes you honest.

I'M NOT A SMART MAN

To those of you who consider yourself to be more than average when it comes to intelligence, can you see yourselves marrying someone who's not? Could you hook up with a brother who just honestly is not a smart man?

As I write this book I'm dealing with several married individuals who have come to me in what I consider an ongoing mental agony. They hooked up with someone who simply does not have the capacity to stimulate them mentally. If you are a person who is formally educated, well-read, or are just blessed with God-given natural intelligence, the reality is you need to date someone who can hang with you mentally.

Don't dummy down to date! The person may be great looking, they may love the Lord, but they simply can't engage in any other meaningful dialogue with you. You've read Baldwin, Angelou, Socrates, Cone, Thurman, Shakespeare, Frost, and Hemmingway. The deepest thing they've ever read is ESPN The Magazine. I'm sorry, but this person is just not ready for an educated, witty, quick-thinking individual like you. In time, you'll be bored beyond what you can imagine and if you don't possess a reverent fear of God, you will find yourself quite possibly seeking mental stimulation from someone else. This search for mental stimulation from another person can lead to attraction, and this attraction can lead to temptation that will be difficult to resist if you're not spiritually mindful.

Let me make myself clear, I am not saying that you have to hook up with someone with at least as many or even more degrees than you. I am not saying the person has to have an IQ out of the roof. No offense, but you might not exactly be a rocket scientist yourself. I'm simply suggesting that you have enough substantive conversations with the person to make sure you are mentally compatible. If neither of you like to read or think, you'll be a great, dumb couple in love. Go for it! Don't compromise in this area; you are going to be with this person until one of you goes to heaven or the Rapture occurs. Make sure you enjoy both talking and listening to them.

So many singles, particularly single women, begin to settle as they get older. They feel that the pool of good, godly single men is limited at best and therefore, if they find a man with a job and Jesus, they grab him quickly and figure out the rest later.

I have counseled several women who were literally in tears because they had said "I do" to somebody who could not...could not turn them on mentally, could not have a deep involved conversation with them, could not relate to them when they needed it most. They describe it as feeling like you're married to a child and being insufferably lonely even while in your spouse's presence.

RIDE OR DIE

Recently, I procured my motorcycle license. I just turned 40 and I think I was having a midlife crisis when I made the appointment to take the test. No, I'm joking. The truth is, I bought my oldest daughter a scooter for her 16th birthday and I decided to get two more so that my wife and I could ride with her from time to time. Between me finishing my doctorate, my wife having and raising babies, and my daughter's crazy school and work schedule, none of us ever went and got our motorcycle licenses. Consequently, the bikes sat in my garage for over three years.

One morning, I decided I was ready to ride. I called to find out what I needed to do to get my license and then spent about a day and a half studying for the test. I scheduled and took the exam and after I received my results indicating I had passed, I did what I always do when something great happens in my life; I called my girl. She was happy and celebrated my accomplishment with me. That same day I went and bought a new helmet and started rolling. Would you believe the very next weekend I received a text from my wife and it was a picture of her motorcycle license? This girl, without telling me, had studied for and passed both her written and driving test. She was not going to let me roll without her. We ride or die together!

Victory Vernon is, without question, my best friend. We have philia in common, meaning we share a loving friendship. We talk about theology, politics, psychology, and everything in between. (I wish I could add sports but I'd be lying; nobody's perfect). We pray together, travel everywhere together, make a lot of love together, and now we ride motorcycles together! I love being married because I married somebody I connect with. We connect on so many levels that we're never bored with one another; nor do we desire the company of another man or woman. I've never come close to cheating because I love what I have at home.

I am a pastor, Bible student, and seminary professor, and I've been saved for a quarter of a century, but every time I look at my wife, I go crazy with lust, which lends credence to my first rule once again; there must be physical attraction. Sometimes I don't know what I thank God for the most—my home or my wife's body. I enjoy her physically and the real beauty of it all? Our physical and sexual connection is biblically supported.

Proverbs 5:19 - She is a loving deer, a graceful doe. Let her breasts satisfy you always. May you always be captivated by her love.

This is one of several references the Bible makes to the splendor of holy sexuality, which is rooted in your connectivity and compatibility. When I feel supported and respected, I am tremendously attracted to my wife. Conversely, when she feels loved and appreciated, she is attracted to me. Thus, our sexual chemistry is often (but not exclusively) cultivated in our mutual respect for and commitment to meet each other's emotional and mental needs. We would have very little desire to fulfill each other, on any level, if we didn't have the compatibility and connectivity that I believe is necessary for any relationship to thrive or even survive.

Here is another reason why Rule 2 is essential: when my philia is not working, when my eros dwindles because of the incessant weariness that sometimes accompanies my busy life, my agape—the love that I have for my wife that is grounded exclusively in the love of God that I possess because of my Christian core—takes over and our relationship continues to flourish, despite any other circumstances.

Even though you need to have some things in common in order to have a solid relationship, you don't have to be exactly like the person you marry. Who needs two of you in the house? It's true that opposites often attract. My wife is short; I'm tall. She hates talking in the morning and I'm wide eyed and excited at 6 a.m. She's patient; I'm aggressive. I could give you another 20 areas in which we are polar opposites, but that said, we connect.

Differences are fine as long as those differences don't keep you from connecting. Believe it or not, there are introverted people who are madly in love with people who won't shut up! One talks all day, the other sits there and listens and they both love it. As long as both are satisfied with what they are getting it's fine. You don't need someone perfect because no one is; what you should pray for is the person that is perfect for you. Pray for God to send you someone you are compatible with—someone you can really see yourself conversing with and enjoying for the rest of your lives. Make sure you connect not only physically and spiritually, but mentally and emotionally also.

You'll be glad you did.

Rule 3: There Must Be Compatibility And Connectivity
Critical Thinking Points

RULE 4

DISCUSS EACH OTHER'S PAST

In my preparation for this book, I spent countless hours asking God to show me the most important ten things singles should know about dating, and also prayerfully considered the order in which I listed them. The first three things I've given you don't take long to discover, and in some cases all three can be detected in one encounter. Think about it. Rule 1 is: There must be physical attraction. For most people (men especially), either you liked what you saw right away or you didn't. Rule 2 is: They must love Jesus. In most cases, just like game knows game, saved knows saved! The average Christian, who has a sound relationship with God knows and can sense quickly when they are in the presence of another believer.

Rule 3 is: There must be compatibility and connectivity. Again, I would argue that it doesn't take too many conversations to recognize a mental connection. Either we click or we don't. By no means am I suggesting that one, two, or even ten conversations will reveal everything about the person. For example, I've been married well over a decade now and I'm still trying to figure this girl out! At the same time, I can state emphatically and without hesitation that I knew I connected with her on our first date.

When we get to Rule 4, things should already be getting serious. Why should I reveal the details of my past to someone who will soon be part of it? You missed that! If this person does not have the potential to be my spouse based on the first three rules, then why reveal the often painful, or if nothing else, private details of my life? Don't start discussing your past relationships, home of origin issues, or anything else with this person unless you're really sensing a godly connection.

Once you feel this person has at least the potential to be your spouse based on the first three rules, it's time to get down to business. Dr. Vernon, why do you call it business? I'm glad you asked!

As a believer (and hopefully a potential believer to those reading this who aren't saved) you don't have time to play. Most people reading this have played enough already and that's why you bought this book. Dating for a Christian is serious business! You need to know a person's past to get a sense of how that can potentially affect your future with them.

HOME OF ORIGIN ISSUES

It is highly critical that you find out how a potential mate was raised and what their family's values were. First, were they reared in a two-parent home and were the two parents biological? More than that, did their parents believe in and honor God in front of them? If the answer to one or more of these important questions is no, it doesn't mean the deal is off, but at least you know who and where they come from. It's naïve to think that what a person saw and experienced as a child won't have some bearing on their conduct as a husband or wife.

For instance, if the woman you're considering had the love of a godly father who prayed for, protected, and affirmed her all her life, most cases, her perception and expectations of you as a man is going to be far different from a woman who has dealt with abuse or abandonment from her father. How could they not? Saved as she may be, she's still human.

If the man you like comes from a home where dad was missing and mom was unfit, how does he know how to love you properly? What model is he using? In many cases, both parents were present and in church and the homes were still unhealthy, which can make church kids grow up and resent God, or at least become indifferent toward Him.

Has the man or woman you like been molested by one or more people, and how has that affected them emotionally, mentally, and sexually? Have they been neglected or suffered abuse in any form? As painful as these dangerous memories must be, I would want to know these things early in the relationship.

TO CLEAN OR NOT TO CLEAN

Were you raised in an environment where you had to clean up or be killed? What if your potential spouse is perfectly comfortable in a home that looks like it's suffered the effects of a tsunami because they don't like cleaning? You might want to discuss that. Of course there are millions of neat freaks who are happily married to slobs. Just make sure you talk about each other's cleaning habits so you know what to expect.

BON APPÉTIT

Another thing you may want to discuss early is what the person's eating habits and expectations in the kitchen are.

MEET THE PARENTS

Did your mom cook and clean everyday while your dad paid all the bills? Is that the model you not only respect, but expect? So many married couples have sat in my office disgusted with their spouse because he or she is the opposite of the parent they grew up idolizing for their tremendous work effort, homemaking skills, etc.

I have two girls and I'm already concerned for my future sons-in-law whom I haven't even met. I have loved, protected, and provided for these girls their whole lives; there is no way they are going to be happy with some lazy guy who won't work or love them properly. All they know is love, protection, and provision. There is tremendous pressure for their potential mates to live up to the standard they are accustomed to.

Every person is different; some come from a life of pain and sorrow and you have to be willing to accept that and love them through it. Others, like my girls, come from a balanced, loving home where a godly mom trained them to be wives and mothers and their father loved, disciplined, and yes, in some ways even spoiled them. Some men, understandably so, want to feel like they are providing a life for their wife she never would have had without him. Can you handle a woman who loves you but doesn't need you to survive financially because her father handled that already? Can you deal with being in his shadow your entire marriage? What if he's a "mommy's boy" and has to talk to his mother every day? Can you handle that, or do your past issues require that you not have to share him with any other woman, including his mother?

I could go on and on about home of origin issues and realities. The point is, there should be a serious conversation about how the person you're interested in was raised and how that could affect your married life together.

THAT'S TOO MUCH INFORMATION

The majority of people reading this book are probably a long way from being virgins. If you happen to still be one by the way, know that there are millions of individuals that would pay money and give up virtually every material blessing they have to go back to that place of innocence. God's best for you is to keep yourself sexually pure until marriage. In doing so you avoid unhealthy soul ties, harmful comparisons, early pregnancy, disease, heartbreak, hurting God, and a bunch of mess that most non-virgins reading this book can relate to.

Those who have had sex before marriage, either by choice, or worse, have had their virginity stolen from them by some very sick person, are forced to deal with all the emotional, physical, mental, and spiritual debris that premarital sexual encounters leave in their aftermath.

To all young people reading this and also to adults that have had the discipline to remain sexually pure, don't give it away! You will be so glad on honeymoon night that you have nobody to compare your spouse to. As a matter-of-fact, no matter how good or bad the sex is that night, it will be the best you've ever had. Wow!

To the rest of you reading this who have had one or more sexual partners, it is what it is! You cannot undo what is done. If you are Christian, the blood of Jesus has washed your sins away and the Bible says you are new in Christ. That said, your past is still your past. Even though you've been forgiven, your past doesn't change. As this new relationship you're considering starts to get serious, it's time to ask one of the scariest and hardest questions you'll ever have to ask this person you like: HOW MANY PEOPE HAVE YOU SLEPT WITH? It's important that you know who and what you're dealing with.

I would hate to be married before I find out that my wife and mother of my children used to be a stripper. I think I'd rather learn of her pole experiences early in the game. Again, I'm not saying it's a deal breaker, but I would like to know if my future husband slept with my sister, or even worse, my mom!

So many people don't ask enough questions before they say "I do." If I'm going to spend the rest of my life with this individual, I don't want any surprises regarding past relationships. I want to know what I'm walking into so I can make an informed, intelligent choice regarding proposing to someone that slept with the entire high school football team.

My advice as a pastor is that you have a "tell all" conversation. Just sit down one day and let it fly! Begin by saying, "Tell me every single person you've slept with or had any sexual encounter with in your life." Now how much detail you want is up to you, but I would at least ask how many.

I would also want to know the intensity of each relationship. How many were one night stands, and how many were heartfelt? How many people have you been in love with or at least thought you were in love with at the time? Have you had two women in the bed at the same time? What about three? What about four? These questions may seem rough, but heck, this is your future we're dealing with! The purpose of these tough but necessary questions is to give you a crystal clear perspective on who you're getting involved with.

If a person has slept with one or more people, there is a strong possibility that there will be comparisons and comparisons aren't just limited to sex. If you've been with anyone before and you didn't sleep with them, chances are you may find yourself comparing the way a former boyfriend or girlfriend acted in certain situations to the way the person you are presently dating does. However, if both of us are saved and have worked through our past mess by attending a Bible-teaching church that offers small groups and good Christian counseling, certainly we can overcome and deal with each other's past mistakes. But sexual history is still worth discussing at the beginning. There are some great people in this world who just don't qualify for a future with you because of their past and that's fine.

Be very picky when it comes to who and what you want in life. The Bible says that God will give you the desires of your heart. If you desire a person that has no children, which we will discuss in the next chapter, then wait on the man or woman who has never fertilized or conceived. If you want a person who is financially stable, which we will discuss in chapter 9, then wait on that person; don't settle for less because you're lonely. If you don't want a person who has had multiple sex partners even though you have, that's still your choice.

Ask the hard questions up front, be prepared to deal with some tough answers, make a firm decision on how you are going to proceed, and follow through on it.

Rule 4: Discuss Each Others Past Critical Thinking Points

_____

_____

_____

_____

_____

_____

_____

_____

_____

RULE 5

DISCUSS CHILDREN

Like it or not, in the 21st century, the average single person in their mid-twenties or older already has at least one child, and in many cases more. If statistics regarding single parenthood are true, then it's likely that well over half of the singles reading this book will date someone with children or are parents themselves. With that in mind, I think it's only intelligent that we discuss it. I remember when I was single, many, many moons ago, a friend and I decided that we would make a commitment to never entertain a woman who had children. If we saw a woman we were interested in, we would ask her in the first five minutes of a conversation, "Do you have any children?" If she replied, "Yes," we would immediately and politely find a way to end the conversation.

We were determined not to marry women who already had children. We were saved young brothers looking for wives, not just someone to sleep with for awhile, so we dated with purposeful intent. I can't stress enough how serious a Christian single should take dating. You should already have your prerequisites in place before you consider someone. Through prayer, you should know exactly what God has called you to deal with and not deal with.

If you're the type of person who just doesn't want to deal with a child you did not make, you are not selfish. You are entitled to set your own standards for who you date. You are under no obligation to do it if God has not called you to it. Somewhere between rules 1 and 4, ask the person if they have children. Women, ask the man you like if there are any children in this world that might be his. You don't want any surprises later, if they can be avoided. Find out if the possibility of him having a child he is not currently aware of exists, however small that possibility might be, and if he is willing to investigate. If the answer to either of these questions is yes and you don't want to deal with it, like my friend and I used to do to women with children, politely and quickly find a way to end it. If you know you don't want, or even more importantly are not called to a person with children, why pursue it any further? I don't care how sexy they are, how saved they are, or how rich they are, if you don't want to raise someone else's child, don't settle!

A DIVINE ASSIGNMENT

Unless God inspires me to do something different, the next book I plan to write will be titled, *Raising Somebody Else's Child: A Divine Assignment*. You might be wondering why I would and what qualifies me to write such a book. I said earlier that my friend and I promised we would never hook up with women with children. Well, to his credit, he kept his word and married a wonderful woman with no children. As for me, I lied! I am happily married to the finest, most beautiful, God-loving, hardworking, supportive, sexy, two-babies-having (when I met her) woman in the world! That's right; I fell in love with a woman who had children when I met her.

Our love story is a long one and you might want to read my first book and autobiography titled, *Blessing Behind Closed Doors* if you want the details, but let me give you what's important for you as a single now. The reason I ended up marrying someone with children is not because I was looking for someone like her, but rather God assigned me to her. I'm 100 percent sure I'm supposed to be married to Victory Rose Vernon and no one else. God sent her to me. If you ask the thousands of people who attend our church they will tell you that no one else in the world is supposed to be my wife and their first lady; we are a match divinely orchestrated by heaven's Conductor.

I adopted the term "divine assignment" to describe the obligation one should feel toward the children of a person they are considering marrying. This unequivocal undertaking, raising someone else's child, should be considered as great a promise as any you will ever make, and should be made with great caution. I regard the choice to take on someone else's child to be a spiritual obligation; thus you should never hook up with someone with children unless God tells you to—hence the expression, divine assignment.

The best scriptural reference I've discovered regarding divine assignment is found in Matthew 1:18-21, when an angel from heaven tells Joseph that his fiancée, Mary, is pregnant. The problem is, he's never slept with her, and she told him she was a virgin. We all know that she was pregnant by the Holy Spirit and she was carrying our Lord and Savior. The point is that Joseph was told by the angel not to get rid of Mary but to help her raise a child he didn't make; in that sense Joseph was given a divine assignment.

I know experientially that there are people with children who would make you a much better spouse than some folk with no kids. If you feel like my buddy and I felt about the no kids rule, you might be asking why in the world somebody would choose a person with kids when there are so many great singles with no children.

Let's say you went to a car lot to purchase a vehicle and there were two identical cars sitting there. The cars look exactly alike except for one clear difference. One has a flat tire. The question you might ask is why anyone in their right mind would choose the one with a flat over the one with no flat. Well, you may not at first, but further investigation reveals that the one with the flat may have a better engine and fewer miles on it. There are some people who have no children but they are selfish and inconsiderate. There are others who may have made mistakes in the past, or perhaps their spouse died and left them with a child; that doesn't mean they would not make a great husband or wife. Remember, the car with the flat tire may have such a great engine, that the flat tire is worth dealing with, and if it has fewer miles, it may be well worth it. Just because a person doesn't have any kids doesn't mean they have a sexually pure past. They may have slept with more people than a person who has children. A real question worth asking is, "How many abortions and/or miscarriages have you had?" Or, to a man, "How many babies have you paid to get rid of?" Again this is tough but real stuff!

I am not by any means attempting to influence you to marry or not marry someone with children; again, that should be based on God's will for your life. I'm simply suggesting that you seek God in this area and be clear about your marriage assignment. If you don't have a divine call to raise someone else's child, then don't even date someone with a child. Right after you ask them if they are saved, ask them if they have a child. If they answer yes, be godly enough to not lead them on. Cordially put an end to the conversation and move on.

If you do decide to date someone with children and find yourself falling for them right away, there are some important things you should understand and do quickly.

MEET THE CHILDREN

It is imperative that you meet and like the children you're going to spend the rest of your life dealing with. However, allow me to insert a disclaimer here for all singles with children: Don't let the person you're dating anywhere near your child until you're certain that God's hand is at work. Children don't need to meet the man of the month; they only need to meet people who have a real chance of becoming their new parent.

When you expose your child to the person you're dating, a bond will likely form between them and that person. They'll observe your fondness of the person and will develop a liking for them as well. The object of your affection will probably be very friendly to your child, as they should be, but perhaps even more than normal to make a good impression on you, thus the child is even more drawn to them.

If the relationship doesn't work out, not only are you affected, but your child is too. Based on a decision that was made through no will or control of their own, they are forced to try to process the emotions of being separated from someone they've developed a bond with. In most cases, they are already grieving one of their biological parents not living with them; the last thing they need is more abandonment issues. As a single parent, be very careful with who you let into their world. If you meet a person and you just don't sense any connection or ability to love their children, move on quickly! Somebody has to go and it's not going to be the kid, so that leaves you.

MEET THE PARENTS AGAIN

In the last chapter, I informed you that you have to learn about the home of origin issues of the person you're dating, including how their parents raised them. That means you need to meet the parents of whoever you love and figure out if they were reared in an environment that is conducive to what you desire for the rest of your life. Well, if you hook up with somebody with a child, you have to meet another parent—the child's biological father or mother. Sorry, but there is no way around it. If you're going to marry this person and help raise their child, you must know all third parties involved. If the child's father or mother is a fool, then you have to determine if the person you are considering is worth the headache of dealing with their child's crazy mother, gangster daddy, or whatever the case may be.

Once you say, "I do," there is no turning back for a Christian unless you have biblical grounds for divorce. I know the Bible pretty well and the last time I checked, "I'm sick of baby momma drama" was not a biblical reason for divorce. Don't get stuck in a marriage before you realize you are not built to deal with another grown person about what's happening in your home. No one really wants to meet or be around someone who has slept with and has a child with the person you love; and by no means am I suggesting you become best buddies—that's actually rather creepy to me—but like it or not, you must meet this person and pray about whether you can deal with them the rest of your life or at least until the children are grown and gone.

BE FRUITFUL BUT DON'T MULTIPLY

A great question for you to ask your potential new spouse is how many kids they want to have. Don't minimize that question. Through this book, you are benefiting from my experience with counseling hundreds of married couples in my church who didn't have these ten rules to guide them. I can't tell you how many couples I know and love who are miserable because one wanted eight kids and the other wanted just one. I know wives who went to the doctor and had their tubes tied without telling their husbands—imagine what that does to the trust level of a marriage. People do change, and sometimes what you didn't want initially shifts with time and experience, but at least try to come to some reasonable number that both of you agree to before you make the marriage commitment.

Rule 5: Discuss Children
Critical Thinking Points

_____

_____

_____

_____

_____

_____

_____

_____

RULE 6

TALK ABOUT MONEY

Do you know that issues related to money are one of the foremost causes for divorce in the country? Most people decide to get married without a concrete financial plan. For one reason or another, they neglect to talk about the interpersonal dynamics related to money; consequently, they leave their financial situation, and their relationship, to chance. Couples think that if they just ignore it, don't talk about money and love each other enough, their finances will work out effortlessly and effectively, as if their money has a will of its own.

Believing that your money issues or concerns will just work themselves out is a gross misconception assumed by many. In reality, however, finances do not just work themselves out! In all probability, without a solid plan for how you will handle money, financial troubles will likely arise. In fact, these troubles tend to increase when not handled aggressively and appropriately. You both can save yourselves years of pain and stress by engaging in candid conversations regarding your views, beliefs, thoughts, and plans concerning this important subject.

Given the artificial nature of relationships in the very beginning—you know, when you're still trying to impress them and they're still not being completely real with you about some embarrassing habit they have—money is probably not a good first date subject. However, if you've been dating awhile and the relationship is becoming more and more serious, it's time to get down to business. I do not mention the word business as an aside. Dating is a business for the committed Christian; it is not a game. When you're looking for your spouse, the person who's going to help you raise a family, it's all about decisions. The quicker you determine that the individual you're dating is not a part of your future, the quicker you can decide to make them a part of your past.

Money is as important an issue as any to discuss before marriage. If you and the person whom you're dating value two completely divergent views related to money and its significance in your lives, these varying views will inevitably lead to disagreements. I often refer to these disagreements and arguments as "heated fellowship." Discussing each aspect of your respective financial situations before marriage, will lessen the heated fellowship you engage in regarding the subject, after marriage. An open and honest conversation is crucial.

As a woman, ask yourself how much money you feel you need to be happy. If you've come from a home where your father took care of all your mother's financial needs, then that's what you're going to expect and in most cases, long for. If you were raised in an environment where your dad was absent, leaving your mother with sole financial responsibility, then your views may be different. Maybe you expect or are determined to earn a living alongside your spouse for fear that the man you are with might someday leave too. Subconsciously, rather than believing in the longevity of marriage, you may find yourself preparing for what you perceive as the inevitability of divorce. Or, perhaps you went to school, are enjoying the rewards of a fulfilling career, and want to continue to work to help your husband build a solid, financial future for the betterment of your family. Maybe you have a higher earning potential. The important thing is to be honest regarding your true thoughts, opinions, and emotions and listen carefully to the way your potential spouse feels.

As a man, ask yourself this question, can you handle your wife earning more money than you? Well, like it or not, my brother, in many instances, Sister-girl will have more degrees than you. This may lead to her earning more money than you. That shouldn't intimidate you, though. She really doesn't need you for your money; she needs you for your ministry! Can you handle that?

Various life experiences often tend to shape one's opinions and views concerning money. For example, is your family wealthy? Have you become accustomed to the finer things in life? Did you previously date someone who legally or maybe even illegally had a lot of money and bought you extravagant things? Is that one of the reasons that you not only desire these things, but expect them as well from anyone you intend to marry? These are serious questions you must pose to yourself.

After sitting in countless sessions with married couples who were experiencing major trouble because they did not discuss money up front, once again, I can assure you that it is one of the most important conversations you should have before you say, "I do."

SHOW ME THE MONEY

When engaging in conversations about money, one of the first points to discuss is how much money each of you have presently. The answers that you both provide should not include your financial vision statements, or how much money you plan to have in the future; this should be a straightforward response indicating your present worth. You each need to know what the other's money looks like right now! In order to see money matters for what they truly are, show each other current bank statements, and any other statements revealing your financial status. Bank statements not only prove how much money you currently have, they demonstrate spending habits. Learning the spending habits of others will tell you tons about their life in general. Too often couples adopt this model: united we stand, divided we bank; while the right approach should be: it's yours, mine, and ours (Todorova, 2008). Honesty is critical when discussing your current financial circumstances. Make sure that you each know the real deal.

One of the most important statements I can make to you as a single person is this: Don't just marry potential, marry reality! It's fine to see the potentiality of an individual, supporting and encouraging them to attain all God has for them. But the reality may be that as of now, he's broke! Are you OK with that? Show each other actual earnings statements. Establish trust at the beginning of your relationship with what you are willing to reveal, because what you don't reveal will affect you in the future.

If the person has had financial issues in the past, do not ignore it. If the person has a shaky employment history at best, don't think that marrying you is going to change their work ethic. It's not that they can't change; however, you must remember that you are not marrying potential, you are marrying the reality. If a man has not demonstrated the ability or willingness to stick with a job, weigh that considerably. Don't marry potential, marry reality. That's who he is. If a woman is not willing to do anything outside the home and expects you to take care of her like her father or previous boyfriends, that's who she is. It doesn't matter how kind, handsome, or sexy they are! None of that pays a mortgage. How much money does the man that you plan to marry currently have? Is the woman you like financially responsible, or does she have a ton of debt? Are you concerned with the answer?

As a woman, you must ask yourself if you're OK with being the sole breadwinner, or at least splitting financial responsibility of the bills accrued. If you are OK with this, that's fine. Just ensure that this fact is discussed, determined, and accepted at the beginning. As a man, if you expect the woman you marry to assist with any financial expenses, let her know up front, while you're dating. There should be no surprises concerning either of your financial viewpoints. Learn what you both think about earning potential. What are the balances in savings and checking accounts? What types of investments have you made? Do you have life insurance policies? How much money goes into your 401K? Lay your financial cards on the table. What should each person produce in the marriage?

Of course, as a Christian, the Bible is pretty clear that God expects every grown person to produce something. "Even while we were with you, we gave you this command: "Those unwilling to work will not get to eat" (2 Thessalonians 3:10).

My wife hasn't worked a job in the traditional sense in well over a decade. Nevertheless, she is active and accomplishes something everyday. Five days a week, she's awake by 6:00 a.m., working out, staying healthy, keeping her body tight for me; she is the primary caregiver for our three youngest children, taking care to make sure they are prepared for their day. Additionally, she assists me in leading thousands of people in our ministry, and furthermore, she loves me, makes love to me as often as I need it and more, while ensuring that our relational connection stays strong. She is the epitome of a woman who "produces" on a daily basis. We discussed these things before marriage; that is, what we each would be responsible for producing.

Years ago, the decision was made that I would be responsible for earning the money, so that my wife could focus on taking care of our family and our home. Again, in the eyes of some, this may not be considered work as it is usually defined. However, my wife is the personification of work; she works the house! In contrast, I make the money. That's our agreement. You too must come to an agreement with the person whom you are seeking to become your spouse.

Do not minimize the importance of discussing each other's expectations. What do you expect your partner to provide or offer, financially or otherwise? If your plan is to be a stay-at-home mom until your children are older, sans traditional employment, that means you need a husband who pays all the bills. What material sacrifices are you willing to make so that you can afford to live on a single income? Really, can either of you afford to stay at home? Settle on if you are both going to be employed. Decide how much money will be saved each month. Agree on investment amounts. Make clear views related to life insurance for the security of your family. Resolve the amount that will be put away for children's college education.

Speaking of children, who in the relationship has children from an outside partner? If either or both of you do, there are child support payments and possible arrearages to consider. Ascertain the sum of debts you both owe. Now is the best time to discuss these issues, not after you have committed to stay together forever.

GIVE ME SOME CREDIT

In no shape, form, or fashion, would I marry someone without seeing their credit report. I know that's personal, but get over it! If I'm going to marry a person, then I need to know who they are. Like it or not, your credit report is a reflection of your past choices. To some extent, it speaks to decision-making skills. Remember, there is a difference between a credit report and a credit score. A credit report is defined as detailed information regarding credit history while a credit score measures creditworthiness.

As your relationship progresses in both seriousness and commitment, you must each, literally, lay your credit reports on the table, reviewing them line-by-line. Actually, lay all three credit reports on the table, from each credit-reporting agency. This is crucial so that you can gain a true financial picture. The credit reporting agencies are: Trans Union, Equifax, and Experian.

You need to know what you're getting yourself into from a financial standpoint if you choose to marry your current partner. Looking at their credit report will help you figure this out. When you view the credit report, verify the total amount of debt. What types of debt are listed? Find out how much money has been paid out towards debt. Establish if credit needs to be repaired, and then decide how you would go about repairing it.

Remember, the day you say "I do" it's no longer their credit, it's our credit! What if your potential spouse has such bad credit that it disqualifies you from obtaining your dream home? What if creditors pursue your finances due to the unpaid debt of your spouse? Sometimes, as much as you may like a person, their past may disqualify them from becoming an integral part of your future. If you've worked hard and done all the right things to appropriately set up your finances, are you positive you want to hook-up with someone who has not done the same? Why would you choose to attach yourself to someone who exhibits no financial discipline? It's almost senseless to pay every bill on time, save your money, make great investments, then forever tie yourself to someone who displays no financial responsibility. Their financial irresponsibility may have reaped monetary brokenness in the form of poor credit. Is this truly someone you envision building a life with?

I'm not saying that there is no way you two can build a life together. What I am saying is that you must make sure it's God who has ordained your union. Don't be blinded by an ample behind, my brother. Trust me, there are plenty of well-endowed women with good credit; good credit speaks to a good name. The Bible says in Ecclesiastes 7:1, (NRSV) "A good name is better than precious ointment…"

Men by nature are turned on by sight. Don't let your sight keep you from seeing! It doesn't matter how gorgeous a woman is; do not choose a life partner solely on Jesus and physical beauty. If a woman has no respect for money, she will spend all of yours and then some. You'll feel as if you're working hard and accomplishing nothing. If her credit report says she's irresponsible, believe it! Remember, you are who you are until you change.

Now, if the person you're dating has made mistakes in the past, but the report shows they have been at least attempting to pay their creditors, this speaks to a new pattern of behavior. A credit report will provide you with your credit history. A credit score is a numerical summary of the information in your credit report. Despite what some may think, credit can be repaired.

You can be understanding towards each other's life mistakes, but remember, this is your life we're talking about. Your potential spouse must demonstrate that they are choosing to improve their financial outlook by addressing any credit issues that they have gotten themselves into. This speaks to integrity and character. Addressing these issues will help to avoid being stuck in a big financial mess.

NO DEBT

One of the smartest things I've ever done was pay off every debt I amassed before I chose to get married. I was a 27-year-old man determined to buy my wife a home to live in before we got married. In order to be approved to buy the home, I was required to handle my prior debts first. I began using nearly half my weekly paycheck to pay off all my bad debt. When I married my wife, I owed no man anything, with the exception of the home I'd recently purchased. Knowing the things I know now, I would not have even borrowed the initial cash for our home. I'd have rather rented until we were able to pay for the house in full.

Debt is demonic! I really want all singles reading this to consider what you and your future spouse could accomplish for God, your family, and each other if you had absolutely no debt. Don't be the average, young, newlywed couple who gets into massive debt from the very beginning of their marriage. Stay away from expensive apartments you can't afford. You may want to buy a home with cash, however this is most often unrealistic. Focus on purchasing a house within your means. Be patient when considering big purchases. Don't take out a huge loan. Instead, save a substantial down payment; this will lower the monthly obligation.

After you've finished reading this book, in conjunction with the Bible, read *The Total Money Makeover* by Dave Ramsey. In the book, he discusses the power and benefit of being debt-free in your marriage, as well as how sacrificing now will permit financial flexibility in the future. Ramsey says, "If you live like no one else, later you can live like no one else."

Ask any well respected married couple, and most will tell you that they wish they had no debt. Wouldn't that be a wonderful way to begin your lives? Know that it is possible and attainable. In order to be debt free, establish the current, total amount of your debt. Start by paying off the small amounts of debt first. When the small amounts are paid off, you can put the funds you were using to pay those debts towards the more substantial debt. Create a monthly budget. Stop impulse buying. Decrease the amount of money you spend on non-essentials every month. Applying these principles can help put your financial futures in perspective.

Realize that along with the joy, marriage in and of itself is going to cause you some headaches and issues too; you can't get around it. Nevertheless, don't let money or the lack thereof add to it. Decide right now to be an above-average couple with unlimited finances and limited debt.

WHAT'S THE PLAN?

Before you say "I do," sit down with your partner and create a realistic financial plan for your joint future. I've jotted down a few thoughts in order to point you in the right direction.

1. **Make sure that you know the full extent of each other's financial situation**. Bring all current financial documents to the table. This may include: earnings statements, bank statements, investment portfolios, 401K declarations, documentation of child support commitments, monthly bills, credit reports, medical invoices, total debt, etc. All pertinent financial documentation should be presented. Not only should you be aware of each other's debts, also

become acclimated with each other's assets. Do you own property, cars, or businesses separately? How will you merge assets?

2. After you've established each other's complete financial picture, **wipe out as much debt as you can before the wedding**. Use Ramsey's *The Total Money Makeover* as a guide. Apply the principles from the book to wisely decrease your joint debt in preparation for your marriage. Also, discuss financial attitudes shaped by upbringing, culture, gender, socioeconomic status, etc. Determine the financial roles for your marriage (i.e., Who will do the majority of the saving? Who is responsible for paying monthly bills?)

3. **Do not accumulate any new debt while attempting to pay for the wedding.** You are preparing for your future. Do so wisely. The wedding is one day in your lives. The marriage will last a lifetime. Set a reasonable budget for the wedding and stick to it. Prepare your mindset for a joint financial future. Do not hide any bank accounts or credit cards. Account for all dollars that will be brought into the household. Concentrate upon building a financially secure marriage.

4. **Decide who will work and settle on it.** Are you both going to be employed? Or is one of you going to stay at home to raise your would-be family? Can you afford to have a spouse who is not employed based on your financial situation? Make sure that these expectations are clear. Discuss past life experiences that shaped current views. Probe to understand long-held financial attitudes, often present since childhood (Nance-Nash, 2011).

5. **Live within your means.** Do not overextend yourselves

financially. Make purchases that you can truly afford. Save in order to make big money buys. Limit the number of credit cards you obtain, as well as credit card purchases. Don't create "bad" debt. Create a monthly budget in order to assist you. Additionally, anything can happen, so plan for emergencies (Todorova, 2011). Based on the present economy, have enough money saved just in case you need to cover your living expenses for an extended period of time.

6. **Buy everything cash or wait to make purchases until you can afford them**. When you want to purchase expensive items or items that may not be in your monthly budget, save for the items, then purchase them with cash. Try to buy only the things that you can truly afford. Save for those things you consider wants.

7. **Save, Save, Save!** Save as much money as you can, as often as you can. Make a savings goal. Be determined to put away cash each month in order to meet that goal. Do not touch money that you have designated for saving. Be candid and realistic with each other regarding the amount of money you're comfortable with saving each month.

8. **Create a five-year financial goal; stick to it**. Envision where you want to be in the future and plan accordingly. Think about each financial aspect of your lives. Make objectives to reach an ultimate goal in each area. For instance, if your goal is to increase your credit score, view your credit reports. Address any inaccuracies contained within the reports. Then, pay off your debt accordingly. As you plan your financial strategy, ensure that there are both short-term and long-term goals.

9. **Help the poor.** The Bible says, "Those who shut their ears

to the cries of the poor will be ignored in their own time of need" (Proverbs 21:13, NLT). Help those people who are less fortunate than you. Give back within your community through your church, or through various community organizations. Volunteer your time to assist at food banks, donate clothes to the Salvation Army, or sow into families you know who need the help. Anyway that you can help the poor, do so.

10. **Tithe at a church you believe in**. Tithing is giving God a portion of what is already His. Tithing demonstrates to God that you trust and believe that He will supply all of your needs. It also helps to show God that your desire is to put Him first. Each person must do just as he has purposed in his heart, not grudgingly or under compulsion, for God loves a cheerful giver (2 Cor. 9:7). When you willingly give God His portion, He is ultimately pleased with that. Tithing is an essential step needed to secure your joint financial future.

Regarding tithing: I wouldn't marry a person who doesn't trust God with their money. Tithing is a spiritual discipline that every Christian should actively exercise. It demonstrates prudence, honor for God, and a commitment to playing one's part in ensuring that the agenda of the church is fulfilled. On the other hand, lack of tithing demonstrates lack of faith, disregard for biblical models of stewardship, and no concern for the fulfillment of godly objectives within the church.

As we conclude this chapter, think of the following: if you decide that you are not financially compatible with your potential spouse, are you ready to endure the consequences if you proceed to marry them anyway? If not, and neither you nor they are willing to change, you each have tough decisions to make. How many people are willing to make tough relationship decisions based on finances?

It's smarter to end a relationship before you're married because you can't get your financial views in-line versus getting divorced because you didn't address financial realities beforehand.

Rule 6: Talk About Money
Critical Thinking Points

_____

_____

_____

_____

_____

_____

_____

_____

_____

RULE 7

PACE YOURSELF/SLOW DOWN

Alright, if you and the person you really like (and by this time, maybe you're starting to consider replacing the word "like" with the other "L" word) have somehow made it through the first six rules and you're still together, then things are starting to get pretty serious. Apparently, there is some major attraction going on here! You're digging the way they look, talk, act, smell, walk, sit, and eat...need I go on? I've been there, and thank God, after years of marriage and a bunch of babies together, I'm still there.

If you've obeyed the rules I've given you so far, this person you're digging is not only attractive to you physically, mentally, and emotionally, but they have a sound relationship with Christ or are at least pursuing one with everything they have. You guys are connecting on most every level and you've already been honest about your past relationships, home of origin issues, and/or idiosyncrasies. You've discussed how and what you feel about each other's children if one or both of you are single parents; if neither of you has a child, you've discussed how many children, if any, that both of you are comfortable having once married.

Things could not be any better right now! The birds are singing, the weather is beautiful, and you're walking around smiling, skipping, and whistling. I would argue that with the exception of a true conversion-to-Christ experience, the feeling that no human feeling can replace—I'm talking being Spirit-filled, experiencing His presence, the works!—there is no greater feeling than the initial feelings of romantic love. What you feel on the inside can only be described accurately by someone currently experiencing it. Those of us that have moved from that initial love to a long-lasting, proven, abiding love held together by Christ and His Word would not trade it for anything, but that does not take away from that warm, crazy, can't sleep, on the phone for six hours, every-song-reminds-you-of-the-person you love that you have when you first fall head over heels for someone.

When you're in love you fall fast—really fast! All of us who have been there know it's not a gradual descent; it's more like jumping off a cliff. It's exhilarating, your heart beats faster than normal when you're with them and you are scared, nervous, overwhelmed, and amazingly happy at the same time. How could anything that feels this darn good possibly go bad?

If I just described the way you are feeling right now in almost exact terms, I have two words for you that could possibly save you from a life of hell on earth. SLOW DOWN! (If you don't feel this way about a person just yet, just remember to revisit these rules when you get to this point). No matter how great this feels right now and I'm sure it does, years of experience counseling hurting couples, has taught me that things are not always what they seem. People put on great acts when they want someone and sadly often reveal their true identity only after getting the ring.

I could name plenty of slick brothers who came in our church and swept one of my precious spiritual daughters off her feet, convinced her to marry him, and then immediately showed his hand. In many cases, he stopped coming to church altogether and made every effort to turn her against me and our ministry. The idea was to get her away from sound biblical teaching and instruction so he could manipulate her and regulate her every move. I have seen women capture and captivate the minds of good sons in our ministry only to marry them and immediately refuse to make love, support, or even encourage them to the extent all husbands need. I have watched with sadness singles who were on fire for the Lord, killing their debt, saving their money, pursuing an education, and purchasing property, throw it all away by marrying the wrong person. If you're sensing passionate pessimism here it's only because I don't want to see you become another negative statistic reflective of a marriage gone bad. My advice to you again is no matter how great things are going right this second, no matter how warm you feel on the inside, slow down and pace yourself.

When you first fall for someone you can't think straight. You're trying your best to balance the rest of your life with what you're feeling, but it is nearly impossible. Everything takes a backseat (including God) when you first fall in love. I believe God understands where you are and He does not hate you for it. Remember, He created not only the agape kind of love that flows from the Holy Spirit, but He also gave Adam and Eve the eros type of love necessary to fulfill each other's needs. It's perfectly natural that some of the time you had devoted to prayer (which we will discuss in Chapter 8) has been replaced with thoughts about this new person in your life. Maybe you even pulled back from some friends and family. To you single parents, the truth is, your children haven't gotten the best you lately because you've been so caught up in this new relationship.

Before you beat yourself up, let me stop you! You are not a bad daughter to your parents, you're not a terrible friend to your buddies, and you are certainly not a bad father to your kid. "Then Dr. Vernon, what am I?" You're in love! I don't want to rob you of what will hopefully be your last time dating anybody and experiencing this new kind of God-based love; I just want to help you gain some perspective and slow things down.

JUST THE TWO OF US PLUS

To single parents, you must always keep in mind that you are not just dating for you; you gave up that right the day you had achild. When you date, you date with you and your child/ children in mind. I don't care how great this person seems to be, your family's well being is at stake. It's now time for you to gather yourself, take a deep breath, and see how your children are responding to this new person in their life. Are they ready for this transition from a one to a two-parent home? Does the person you love have children and are their children going to be visiting or even moving in? Are your kids properly prepared for this whirlwind transition that will inevitably cause them some grief? I know you're thinking, how could this great person coming into our lives possibly cause my child grief? Grief is caused by any change of a normal pattern or behavior in our lives.[1] There is no greater change for a child than having their mother to him or herself and then having to share her with some man who they are unsure if they can trust yet. As a single parent who's been floating the last year or so, it's time to get back grounded and make sure all parties involved are transitioning properly.

TIME OUT

My advice to all singles at this point in the relationship is to back up and take a deep breath. Have you ever heard the old saying, "Sometimes you can't see the forest because of the trees?" Someone flying a helicopter has a much different view of a forest than someone walking through it. The person walking through it can't see the whole forest because they are too close to it. Sometimes you have to step back from something to properly assess it.

When you've reached this level of intensity in a new relationship, trust me when I tell you that you are probably too caught up in it and definitely too close to it to see clearly. My advice to you is to set some real parameters around the times you spend together. At this point you already know that you love them and you're probably going to marry them; thus, it's now time to regain your mental equilibrium and pace yourself.

1. John W. James and Russell Friedman. *The Grief Recovery Handbook: The Action Program for Moving Beyond Death, Divorce, and Other Losses.* 20th Anniversary ed. (New York: HarperCollins, 2009), 57.

Believe it or not, when you're dating, especially as a Christian, there is such a thing as being together too much and too long, which can lead to one of the worst mistakes you can make and that's having sex. (We'll discuss this subject in the next chapter). As hard as it may be, you and the person you have fallen for should both decide to step back and gain some perspective. Following this rule is integral for the future success of your relationship. Things are simply happening too quickly and if you don't slow down you may miss something about the person that you need to discover before you get married.

Enough of the floating for a minute; it's time to get serious about your investigation of who this person is and if you're really spiritually, mentally, and emotionally ready for the changes that come with marriage. This is not just about great sex and someone to go half on the house note with. This is your life we're talking about and you need to be sure this is the person you want to spend the rest of your life with, not just the next six months!

I'LL SEE YOU WHEN I SEE YOU

You should really consider drastically decreasing the amount of time you're spending with this person. I know what you're asking. "How can I truly get to know the person unless I spend quality time with them?" By this point in the relationship, you've probably either been with them, on the phone with them, or texting them every available moment of both of your lives. That lends credence to my point that you've actually probably been together or interacting so much that you haven't had time to think, and most of all, hear God clearly concerning this person. If I were you, I would ask your mate to agree with you to back up and set specific times for seeing each other and even talking on the phone. When you do talk, limit the conversations to discussing business only.

Enough of the fluff stuff; it's time to dig into the details of where you're headed. If you don't go to the same church, you should be discussing where you're going to worship. Who is going to have to say goodbye to their pastor and church family? Is this going to be a problem? What about any past familial or relationship issues? What's the plan for addressing them? And of course, there is the issue of money, which we discussed when we covered Rule 6—what are we doing to address any credit and/or debt issues? We need to talk about any and everything we can think of related to starting and having a life together.

As hard as it may be for two people madly in love to stay away from each other for awhile, it's crucial that you step back and make sure you're not falling too fast and that you are thinking things through. Remember, you're not mad at each other and this is not a break up. You are simply choosing to do what's best for the future of your God-based relationship and hopefully, married life together. You're not average! You are determined to actually pray and think before you jump into something you regret.

Don't be surprised if you begin to identify some things about the person that you don't like so much once you are in a place to think clearly; that's not a bad thing, that's called life! No one is perfect, including you and the person you're falling for. The more of those things you can find out before marriage the better, and trust me when I tell you that even after marriage there are more surprises to come.

Have you carefully considered why you want to get married? Yeah, yeah, yeah, I know you feel like they're "the one," and you've "never felt this way about anyone" and you feel like "it just doesn't get any better," but do you really know why you want to get married? Is it to avoid loneliness? Are you getting older and feeling the pressure to tie the knot soon, for fear that you'll end up an old maid? Are you looking for someone to fill an emotional cavity left by some woman who broke your heart? Are you in a sinful relationship where you're fornicating or incessantly lusting and you want to get married so your sexual immorality is no longer an issue? Have you found a person who meets all your standards and expectations and want to make it official as soon as possible for fear of letting them get away?

If you answered in the affirmative to any of the questions above regarding the reasons why you want to get married, you need to step back for sure, do some more praying, and consider reevaluating your self-worth, your motivation, and your relationship with God before you go any further.

Marriage is a spiritual union. It was designed by God to be representative of His relationship with the church. This uniting of souls—the merging of two persons into one—should embody the idea of a safe, sacrificial, and selfless love, or, the love we enjoy as heirs to the kingdom of God. Marriage is an ever-evolving exercise in unselfishness and a daily challenge. It is a relationship that requires you to often give up your own needs, wants, and desires to meet your spouse's needs, wants, and desires.

By now, as the premise of Rule 2 is a recurring theme in almost every chapter, you know how strongly I feel about the importance of the person you're considering marrying being saved and Spirit-filled. But, I don't want to misguide you into believing that just because the two of you are saved your marriage will be perfect, or even anything remotely close to it. Regardless of how saved you both are, the ultimate reality the two of you must face is that you are marrying a sinner. There will be days when your spouse, despite his or her love for God and for you, will disappoint you, anger you, frustrate you, and yes, even hurt you. As you breezily ambulate through the corridors of love's abode, you must strive to keep a level head and an open, spiritually conscious mind. What you must always be mindful of is that the person you are marrying will inevitably fail to meet your expectations to some degree—some degrees more intense than others.

You need a calling to your spouse that exceeds your "love" for them in order to have a successful God-centered marriage. At some deeply intrinsic level, your commitment to your spouse needs to be completely, totally, and utterly encapsulated in your belief that God Himself is the nexus of your connection. Your focus, especially by this juncture in your dating experience, should be exclusively on determining if this relationship is in God's will for your life, and more specifically, your future marriage.

Marriage will bring with it sometimes seemingly insurmountable obstacles. Your faith and your spirit will be tested immensely by your spouse's (and your own) sinful nature. If God is not the superior reason for your marriage; if your happiness is more important to you than your holiness; if your personal agenda is more important to you than honoring the spiritual union that you chose to commit to, in difficult times you will be faced with an alternative that is far more attractive than remaining in a relationship that at times causes you insufferable stress. That alternative, I can tell you, is not God's will for your marriage. If marriage is to symbolize Christ's relationship with us, the Church, then breaking your marriage covenant would imply that God's relationship with us can too be broken, and where would the safety and security of a loving God be in that? Of course, there are exceptions, but those exceptions do not include, "I've fallen out of love," "this is not what I thought it would be," or "this is too much work." Marriage is unlike any of your other previous relationships, where you could jump in and out at will. It is a lifelong, loving, commitment. Consider this quote taken from

Gary Thomas', *Devotions for a Sacred Marriage: A Year of Weekly Devotions for Couples:*

> If I am to rid myself of anything that may contaminate body or spirit, then I can give no place in my life to...selfishness. I am always called to practice gentleness, kindness, goodness, faithfulness, and self-control. Someone else's sin—even the sin of my spouse against me—never gives me the license to respond with sin. I am called to just one motivation, and one only: reverence for God. In one sense, what my spouse says or does or doesn't do is almost irrelevant. Every decision I make, every word I utter, every thought I think, every movement I perform, is to flow out of one holy motivation: reverence for God. Are you a God-centered spouse?[2]

Heavy stuff, isn't it? When we take the focus off of our potential mate, and shift it toward its rightful place on God, all of a sudden marriage seems far more or—depending on where you are in your walk with Christ—far less appealing. At the very least it may seem a more spiritually daunting task than you may have originally surmised. However, it is also a unique opportunity, one unmatched by any other relationship we could possibly enter into, to grow closer to God through an experiential understanding of His relationship with us. Of course, His love is a perfect love and ours can never be, but marriage does give us a semblance of how strong and undying Christ's commitment to us must be when we marry a person, deal with their faults and flaws daily, and are forced to forgive those inadequacies in order to maintain our relationship with Him.

A marriage qualified by God's standards has to be entrenched in an unwavering obligation to stay committed to one's spouse, an agreement to love them continually, and an understanding that if my

2. Gary Thomas. Devotions for a Sacred Marriage: A Year of Weekly Devotions for Couples. (Kindle Edition. Zondervan, 2009). Kindle Locations 128-133

spouse does not reciprocate any or all my efforts, it does not give me biblical sanction to end it.

Thomas discusses this even more emphatically in *Sacred Marriage: What if God Designed Marriage to Make Us Holy More than to Make Us Happy?*:

> In a society where relationships are discarded with a frightening regularity, Christians can command attention simply by staying married. And when asked why, we can offer the platform of God's message of reconciliation, followed by an invitation: "Would you like to hear more about that good news of reconciliation?" In this sense, our marriages can be platforms for evangelism. They can draw people into a truth that points beyond this world into the next. Just by sticking it out in our marriages, we can build a monument to the principle and the practice of reconciliation.
>
> Years ago, Paul Simon wrote a best-selling song proclaiming "Fifty Ways to Leave Your Lover." A Christian needs just one reason to stay with his or her "lover": the analogy of Christ and his church.[3]

So you see, this is about more than just "a feeling." It is about more than just being in love. Marriage is serious kingdom business. Are you ready for an undertaking of this spiritual magnitude? Do you feel strongly enough about the person you are dating, and even more importantly, are you rooted enough in God to enter into a marital relationship? If you don't feel you can answer these questions with a 'yes' just yet, it doesn't mean you need to end your relationship. It means that you need to slow down, gain some perspective, and make sure the person is worth the serious sacrifices you will ultimately make.

3. Gary Thomas. Sacred Marriage: What If God Designed Marriage to Make Us Holy More Than to Make Us Happy? (Kindle Edition. Zondervan, 2008), Kindle Locations 542-548.

Rule 7: Pace Yourself/Slowdown
Critical Thinking Points

_____

_____

_____

_____

_____

_____

_____

_____

_____

RULE 8

ENGAGE OR DISENGAGE

It's been truthfully stated that it's easy to get saved because Jesus did the hard part on the cross; however, it's hard to be a Christian. How many of us would be awesome Christians if it weren't for our bodies? Think about it. Paul wrote a whole chapter, Romans 7, concerning how his flesh was always messing him up, and how he had to literally depend on the power of God to keep him right. The majority of single people reading this, over the age of 18, have been in at least one dumb relationship they truly regret. You gave up too much, put up with too much, or went through too much. It is my prayer that your next relationship or the one you're currently in, can and will be different.

There comes a point in Christian dating where you have to decide if you and the person you're with are going to get engaged. Okay, I'll say it again; there is only one reason a Christian should be dating. Christians date to get married. We don't "play" date! Fooling around in the dating department will only lead to premarital sex. It'll also lead to more of the same mess that many of you have already been through; everything from Herpes to heartbreak. The only reason you should go on a second date is if you were totally impressed on the first one. Remember, as soon as you discover that this is not the person you are going to spend the rest of your life with, end the relationship quickly! Christians date to get married! Period! Christians don't date for the sole purpose of having fun, hanging out, or because they're lonely on a Friday night. If you want to do those things, do them with your friends and family. You should never hang around someone of the opposite sex whom you are attracted to. Do not give yourself that much credit; you will end up in the bed! Trust me!

ALL THE SINGLE LADIES

Let's not play games. Men and women are different.

Publishers Weekly reported that women buy more books than men; to the tune of 68% of all books. The reality is that there are probably more women reading this book right now than men. That being said, it is my prayer that every woman reading this would recommend, or buy a copy for some single man in her life whom they care about— an uncle, a brother, or any man they know who needs it.

Throughout my writing process, I couldn't help but think of the thousands of beautiful women that I pastor each weekend. My wife and I stand at the front of the sanctuary after every service each weekend, listening to hundreds of women give us their sad but true stories about the latest man they're dating. Most of the women, like many of you reading this book, are conflicted and convicted at the same time. They feel as if they love this brother, but because they're Christians something just doesn't feel right. In many cases they've already slept with him. Due to the sexual bond, lust is confused with love (which we'll discuss in the last chapter). The men they are dating and/or sleeping with have no idea how to love them. In all probability, the men have most likely never seen a godly man model chivalry, honor, or respect for women.

As you're reading this, think about the men you've dated who weren't right for you. The man may have been solely focused on getting his needs met. His needs could have been sexual, financial, mental, or otherwise. He might have been simply wondering about how you, the woman he was sleeping with, could help him. Oftentimes, he didn't demonstrate that he cared about helping you, it was all about himself. You must remember this though: lust takes, agape love, gives! If a man doesn't know Christ, how can he love you properly? Even if he is saved, it doesn't mean that he knows how to be a husband. Do you know that you can be saved and crazy? (Read the next rule for more details). Most men have no idea what women truly need from them. Therefore, as a woman, you must demand certain things. Demand what you need.

Think about the following: What if my father did not love my mother biblically in front of me? In addition, what if all my brothers, uncles, cousins, and friends used women as objects to get their needs met? If I don't attend a teaching church where the pastor actually teaches men to be husbands and fathers, tell me, as a man, what am I supposed to draw from in order to love a woman properly?

Single mothers, please think about this. It may help you to understand (not excuse) your child/children's father(s) if they are not fulfilling their parental responsibilities. In many cases they don't know how to be good fathers because they've never seen it done right. Additionally, ask yourself why you chose to sleep with someone who had proved nothing, and made no godly commitments to be your husband or your children's father.

When you begin dating a man, it's crucial to ask about his home of origins issues. Did he have a godly father? Does he currently have a great relationship with his mom? Has he ever been molested and/or exposed to sexual deviance at an early age? Did his father abuse or cheat on his mother? This also speaks to the importance of **Rule 4, Discuss Each Other's Past** and the next rule, **Rule 9, Go to Counseling.** Troubling answers to any of the aforementioned questions does not disqualify a man from being a great husband and father in the future. I've witnessed hundreds of brothers in my church, by the grace of God, the power of the Holy Spirit, and biblical teaching, transition from womanizing fools to kingdom husbands and fathers.

However, it's crazy not to do your homework on a man at the beginning of a relationship, before you give him everything. That's right, I said everything! When a woman loves, she loves hard and unreservedly. Women don't know how to half love a man. Women either love a man completely or not at all. R. Kelly said, "When a woman's fed up, there ain't nothin' you can do about it." What he should've said is that when a woman is in love (or confused lust), there ain't nothin' you can do about it! Her momma, her sister, her best friend, and everyone who loves her can try to convince her that the man she loves isn't right for her, but sadly, she won't let him go until the damage is done. Many women reading this can remember a man in their past who they knew was not the one for them; but they loved him anyway. As they look back retrospectively, they try to figure out exactly what they loved. Here are a few things they can ask themselves regarding their time with him.

- Did he pour into you spiritually by praying and reading God's Word with you?

- Did he care about your emotional, physical, and financial well being more than his own?

- Did he love and honor you enough not to sleep with you? If you did have sex, was he truly sorry to God and you for not honoring your temple by waiting until your honeymoon night?

- Single moms, are your children better off spiritually, financially, mentally, and emotionally because you were with him?

Take an honest, deductive look at the situation. In most cases, you were provided with great sex, (which was sin!) and maybe good conversation. Other than the painful lessons you learned from dating a fool, you didn't really get anything out of it. Those of you with children might argue that at least he gave you a wonderful child, although you must realize that any man with healthy sperm could have done that for you. It wasn't God's will for you to get pregnant before you got married; He just loved you enough to bless you through it all.

As a woman, be honest with yourself about your own mistakes. Stop blaming men for everything that's wrong with you, or for where you are in life. With the exception of date rape, molestation, or any other tragic incident that was totally out of your control; take responsibility for the choices you've made concerning men. This includes the one you're dating now or will date in the future. Use the rules in this book to make good, solid choices in your current or next relationship. Either God sent him or He didn't! The quicker you find out the better. This means the less unnecessary drama you'll have to endure.

In Exodus 20, God gave His people Ten Commandments through His main man Moses. I've taken the liberty to give **All the Single Ladies** reading this what I call the **Ten "Demand-ments."** As saved, single women you must demand certain things from yourself and any man you seriously date. I understand that before this book, the word Demand-ments didn't exist, but it does now!

The Ten "Demand-ments" for All the Single Ladies

1. **Demand yourself to love and trust God more than any man.**

2. **Demand yourself to pray, as well as read your Bible consistently.**

3. **Demand yourself to desire the filling of the Holy Spirit more than sex.**

4. **Demand yourself to go to a teaching church weekly; be active in the ministry you are called to.**

5. Demand that any man who approaches you knows or is willing to get to know Jesus in an intimate way.

6. Demand that any man you date honors the God in you and treats you like a kingdom woman at all times.

7. Demand yourself to never allow any man to hit you and still have you.

8. Demand that any man you're considering marrying get as healthy as possible in every way before you say "I do."

9. Demand of yourself that you never settle for any man that God did not send.

10. Demand that from this moment on, no man will ever have sex with you unless he's your husband.

I'm aware that technically you can't demand an adult to do anything they're unwilling to do. But, you can demand what they must do if they want to be with you. Moreover, you must certainly learn to demand things of yourself. I love the way the Bible puts it in 1 Corinthians 9:26 (NLT), "I discipline my body like an athlete, training it to do what it should." Paul is saying in essence to put a **demand** on yourself to do what's right. I don't let my body run me, rather I allow the God in me, to run my body.

A scripture for every sexy girl with no spiritual substance is 1 Timothy 4:7-8 (NRSV): "Train yourself in godliness, for, while physical training is of some value, godliness is valuable in every way, holding promise for both the present life and the life to come." Allow me to modernize, contemporize, and Vernon-ize this piece of the Bible. Paul is saying that to have a beautiful figure because you work out is great, but what good is it to have a sexy shape and still be sad? A great job but no joy? To be popular but still have no peace? Good hair but a bad heart. Nice clothes but ugly character? A master's degree but still masturbating? You can demand from yourself, with the power of God, to be the woman He has predestined you to become. Don't settle for less than the man He wants you have. Don't settle for being less than the kingdom woman He has called you to be.

All My Dogs

I'm sure by now you've noticed that I'm not the average pastor and this is not the average spiritual book on dating. In a sense, I write the way I preach. It's edgy but honest, raw but very real. If you're ever in the Cleveland area, visit one of "THE WORD" CHURCH campuses. One of the first things you'll notice distinguishing "THE WORD" CHURCH from the average church is that thousands of men attend our church. I made the decision years ago, to not have a church full of women only. There's a great book by David Murrow titled, *Why Men Hate Going to Church*. The reality is that mostly women show up at church, supporting the ministry in every way. Due to this situation, most churches and pastors cater to women and what they like to see happen in the church. In addition, most authors cater to women because again, women more often purchase books. It is my prayer that this section in particular, is being read by some sincere single brothers who really want to gain knowledge to become the kingdom men God has called them to be.

Did you notice this section is called **"All My Dogs"**? That's not a typo. Even as a pastor, husband, and father, I too still have some "dog" in me. I'm a full-fledged heterosexual man who loves to look at a woman with a pretty face and a wicked body. Getting saved and spirit-filled did not take that desire away from me. Men, vis-à-vis women, are turned on by sight! Ontologically, anthropologically, theologically, and any other "ly" you want to add, it's just true! We are dogs! Some of us are breast men, some are butt men, some are leg men, and some of us have foot fetishes. More often than not, most of us like all of the above and more on a woman.

Let me clarify for the really "churchy" readers, what I mean by dogs. For years, I've listened to women in my family who were upset with some man they supposedly hated but were somehow pregnant by, talk about how all men were dogs. I was honestly curious about this juxtaposition of men and dogs. I quickly discovered that the reason women call men that is because of the average dog's desire and propensity to sleep with any other female dog he's attracted to. Well, like it or not, the more I thought about it, I had to concur that most men including myself would love to sleep with any woman that has the kind of face and/or body he likes. However, what the women in my family and most women in general fail to distinguish is that there are two types of dogs: trained and untrained. Colloquially, we call the untrained dogs "mutts." Now you might be asking what the difference is. I'm glad you asked! A trained dog wants the same thing an untrained dog wants. The difference is, one has a Master, and the other does not! The only thing that separates me from the average single man reading this book is that I'm scared of and submitted to my Master, Jesus.

STAY ON THE PORCH

Have you ever seen someone walking their female dog down the street? Notice what happens when they walk by a house where there is a male dog sitting on the porch? Everything in that trained male dog wants to do the same thing an untrained, wild dog would do, and that is to jump off the porch and have sex with the female dog as soon as possible. However, as soon as the dog looks like he wants to try something, or starts to make that sound that dogs make when they want to bust a move, his owner simply says one word that kills it all—"Stay!" No matter how much he wants it, the dog's owner said, "Stay, Boy!" That's enough to keep the dog on the porch.

Every single brother reading this book must first reconcile that he cannot control his flesh on his own. He cannot love a woman properly without a power greater than himself. 1 John 4:4, NASB, says "...greater is He who is in you than he who is in the world." God is our Master. He demands that we honor the women in our lives in every way. So, when God tells us that we must "stay on the porch," that's exactly what we must do.

TRAINING DAY

During a prior Black History Month, I preached a message, specifically to black men, titled "Training Day." In the message, I argued that most black men and men in general, have not been trained to be godly husbands and fathers. I've been saying for years that you don't just naturally become a great husband and father. Sex is natural, marriage and fatherhood are not. No one has to teach you how to have sex; God designed us to do it naturally. He also designed a system whereby a man's father and mother are supposed to model love and respect in front of him, so that he naturally perpetuates that godly behavior in his own home.

Many single brothers have been wounding women for years. I can't tell you how many men, even in my church, have admitted to me that they cannot remember all the names of the women they've slept with. Wow! Somehow, they've made it through life with no one ever telling them that men should only sleep with their wives. Maybe no one ever stated to them that they should only get one woman pregnant, have all their children with that woman, and ensure that, that woman is their wife. It takes a greater man to make one woman smile for 30 years, than to have simply slept with 30 women.

One of the many reasons I wrote this book is because I'm convinced that most single men really don't know how to date. Many don't know how to honor a woman. In particular, many men have not learned to stay celibate until marriage; let alone keep their virginity intact. It is countercultural to men to even suggest waiting to have sex until honeymoon night. In the final rule of the book, I'm going to spend ample time dealing with the devastating effects of premarital sex.

However, to all men reading this right now, realize that women have sex differently from men. Men have detached sex. This explains why a good portion of the men in my church don't even remember the names of the women they slept with. It was "just sex" to them. Conversely, I guarantee the average woman reading this book can remember every man that's ever touched her. (It might take some a little longer than others). Most women really want to love and be loved by the man they give themselves to sexually.

As I said earlier, women love harder than men. Some men play off of this fact. It's imperative to understand, the average woman has father issues, or she's been wounded by one or more of the men in her life. If a woman is over 20 years old, chances are she's had at least one child that needs and deserves their father, but can't have him, though every child deserves to have a quality relationship with their father. Add to this, the horrific reality that many women, in my own church too, have been molested by some demonically controlled individual, stealing their innocence. The last thing these women need in their lives is more hurt!

Determine now, that you will honor, in every way, the woman you are currently dating or will date in the future. I'm blessed to have a mother, three beautiful sisters, and two daughters, that I would kill a man over! (Just kidding...no I'm not). I keep it real simple. I treat my wife Victory, the way I would want any man to treat my sisters, as well as my daughters. I really believe that God has thousands of brothers reading this book who don't even go to church. I have a sneaky suspicion that He wants to use you brothers to bless a woman! That's right, bless a woman! My wife is blessed because she met me! She's blessed financially, mentally, but most of all, she's blessed spiritually.

Despite your past issues and circumstances, there is a woman out there that you are supposed to be a blessing to. Men are not in relationships to receive only; they should be giving too. Don't ever worry about receiving from a woman. The majority of women will always give back to you more than you gave to them. It's simply a woman's nature. Men, purpose in your heart to be selfless. Love your would-be wife in the way of Ephesians 5.

Have you ever read that? Ephesians 5:25-33, from the Message Bible states:

"Husbands, go all out in your love for your wives, exactly as Christ did for the church—a love marked by giving, not getting. 26 Christ's love makes the church whole. His words evoke her beauty. Everything he does and says is designed to bring the best out of her, 27 dressing her in dazzling white silk, radiant with holiness. 28 And that is how husbands ought to love their wives. They're really doing themselves a favor—since they're already "one" in marriage. 29 No one abuses his own body, does he? No, he feeds and pampers it. That's how Christ treats us, the church, 30 since we are part of his body. 31 And this is why a man leaves father and mother and cherishes his wife. No longer two, they become "one flesh."

³² This is a huge mystery, and I don't pretend to understand it all. What is clearest to me is the way Christ treats the church. ³³ And this provides a good picture of how each husband is to treat his wife, loving himself in loving her…"

Men don't get married until you're ready to love a woman the Ephesians 5 way. I'm telling you, my friend, no matter what you have been through with women in the past, God wants to bless your current or next relationship if you do it His way. Women need love and acceptance from us in the same way that we need sex and respect from them.

PUT A RING ON IT

I'm sincere when I use the phrase, **Engage or Disengage**. At some point in a relationship, you, as a man, have to decide if the woman you're dating is the woman God placed in your life to marry or not. If she's not the one, leave her alone and let her go. It's better to walk away having never touched her or promised her anything. Remember, the purpose of dating is to get married. Period! If she's not your wife then break it off clean. The quicker the better regarding women. The longer you stay, the more they expect, and expectations are a trip. You can only be hurt by someone you have expectations for. This is why I become so angry with men who mess around with women who were doing fine without them. In most cases, she was serving the Lord, keeping herself celibate, and simply taking care of her business. She wasn't looking for a man. She was looking for God's will in her life. However, soon some guy comes along and approaches her. Because she's human, wanting to give and receive love, she falls for the guy (in most cases too quickly). She goes from a woman perfectly at peace, to a woman in a posture of expectation. Why? Some brother, who had no intentions of marrying her, was just having sex with her (which is just as much her fault) until it no longer excited him, then he dropped her.

Decide now that you will never be "that guy" again. If you've dated a woman about a year, two years at the most, it's time to either Engage or Disengage. Hopefully, you haven't touched her sexually, but even if you have, it's time to be honest with her and yourself. Do you love her enough to marry her? Are you willing to do the work needed to be the man she needs you to be? The man God has called you to be? The longer you both wait to make this decision, the harder it will be. It's always better to make a clean break. Trust me, women appreciate this more than being strung along and used for years.

On the other hand, if you've determined that she is your wife to be, get engaged! Don't procrastinate! Engaged means you're now officially committed. She's off limits to all other men, and you're off limits to all other women. It's the Bible way. It's the right way.

Rule 8: Engage Or Disengage
Critical Thinking Points

.

RULE 9

GO TO COUNSELING

The first two years of my marriage I did not want to come home and my wife did not want me to come home. My parents were young when they had me, and consequently, I spent a lot of time away from them in my formative years. I brought a lot of the issues resulting from the unsettling relationship I had with my parents, unresolved, into my marriage. My wife was a P.K. (preacher's kid) and brought unresolved issues with her from her upbringing. All the details of what we both went through as children and young adults are not as important as the fact that we did not address them properly before we got married.

I'll never forget our first and only premarital session. (It isn't counseling unless the person is a certified counselor, and in our case the person was not). The only advice we were given was to pray and read God's Word. So we went home and prayed, read God's Word, and got married on Valentine's Day just as unhealthy as two people could be. We had no idea how complex the issues were from our childhood, nor were we cognizant of the inevitable corollary of not working through those issues, and we were certainly unaware of how deeply they would affect our marriage. Our imperceptiveness cost us both greatly, because those complications from childhood all came pouring out before the honeymoon was even over. This beautiful woman I had married had some ugly things inside her that she had not properly dealt with, and so did I. The truth is we had gotten married too quickly, needed professional counseling desperately, and could have easily used another year or two of working through our personal issues before the wedding.

After a couple of years, other circumstances in my life unrelated to my marriage, led my wife and I into the offices of Bishop Joey Johnson, founder and senior pastor of The House of the Lord in Akron, Ohio, and my pastor and spiritual covering. Bishop Joey came into my life during a very difficult period at my first ministry. I was unaware at the time, but he was not in my life to help me save my previous ministry, he was in my life to help me save my marriage.

My wife and I were going through an incredibly tough season, and we had no idea how to weather it. Bishop Joey's sage advice, spiritual knowledge, lifelong wisdom, and conciliatory objectivity saved our marriage. He gave us the insight and understanding that we needed so badly prior to walking down the aisle.

Today, we still go to counseling about twice a year, just to keep our marriage intact. We were fortunate that neither of us considered divorce to be an option during that two year period, but we are the exception and not the rule. As arduous as it was for us to just coexist, I am almost certain that another couple in a similar situation would probably have opted to separate rather than put up with the mental and emotional anguish we suffered as a result of our mutual unhealthiness. Plain and simple, we were unhappy. It is far better to expose and deal with your issues before marriage! As a matter-of-fact, not only is it better, it is critical that you go to counseling and uncover or discover whatever issues you or your future spouse have not resolved.

God certainly graced us, and my wife and I are both thankful that He did. Not only has our ability to overcome our early challenges allowed us to be an example for the thousands in our ministry, but I believe He also facilitated our reconciliation to a healthy place in Him because of our assignment to help millions through the writing of this book.

YOU SO CRAZY

Everybody has some stuff that could potentially impinge on their marital happiness. I don't care who you meet and how wonderful they appear; unless they have already done the necessary work of Grief Recovery and a host of other things I'll give you later, trust me, they are not who you think they are.

For years the Judeo-Christian Church has been afraid to conflate spirituality and emotional health, when the two are by no means mutually exclusive. Because I love Jesus does not mean I don't have emotional and mental issues. You can be saved and crazy, just like you can be saved and nasty, saved and evil, saved and depressed, and saved and stupid. Jesus paid the price on the cross so that crazy, nasty, evil, depressed, stupid people could go to heaven. Halleluiah! That said, we still have to do the work to get as healthy as we can as believers. Isaiah 1:5 (NLT) says, "Why do you continue to invite punishment? Must you rebel forever? Your head is injured, and your heart is sick."

God is asking His people why they would continue in the same behavior that's hurt them in the past. He basically tells them, "Your head is crazy and your heart is broken!" Did you notice the question He asked them? "Why do you continue to invite punishment?"

The latter can aptly apply to every woman reading this who dated the same guy over and over again—given they may have had different names and social security numbers, but the same guy in terms of personality, behavioral patterns, his level of respect for you, etc. After each inevitable breakup or revelation that he was sleeping with someone else, in many cases someone you knew or was even kin to, God would whisper the question in your spirit: "Why do you continue to invite punishment?" How many times have you said to yourself, "I'm sick of this mess! I'm through with him and I don't ever want to see him again in my life!" We both know you were back with him by the end of the week only to be devastated over and over again. Again, God would ask you "Why do you continue to invite punishment?"

You know it's bad when a man gets to the point where he knows you're not going to leave him no matter what he does and who he does it with. I even know of a case where the man had been caught and forgiven so much that he finally just told her "Look I'm going to do whoever I want, when I want, and you can stay or go." She stayed and years later he's still doing who he wants when he wants.

Do you know why many of you put up with some things for far too long, things you hate to even remember or discuss? God answers that in Isaiah 1:5, "Your head is injured, and your heart is sick." You were operating from a crazy head and a broken heart. Make sure you highlight or underline this next statement: WHEN YOUR HEART IS BROKEN, YOUR HEAD DOESN'T WORK! That's why those of you who just came out of a hurtful situation should not date anyone or make any major decisions right now; your heart is still broken and your head is not working. If you date someone else while you're still hurting, you won't be able to think clearly. Truth be told, it's really unfair to the person you're rebounding with because all they are is your temporary relationship reefer. You will probably end up in bed with them having anesthetizing sex that will confuse things even further.

So many singles, both men and women, are dealing with grief and broken hearts and don't know it. For many of you, it was mom and dad's mess—either one or both of them were missing, or sometimes even worse they were present and dysfunctional. Many of you are the innocent victims of molestation or premature sexual exposure, which may have confused you sexually and led to lesbianism, homosexuality, or sleeping with whomever wanted you because you felt you had no worth.

When I married Victory, I still had a broken heart. I didn't know it was broken, I didn't know I had not resolved the pain from my past, I didn't know that subconsciously I wanted her to replace all the hugs I didn't get as a child, and maybe even mother me and heal my broken heart from all of my abandonment issues. She had stuff,

I had stuff; it was crazy! If that's not enough, I got her pregnant the first month of our marriage, so we were newly married, emotionally unhealthy, and pregnant. She wouldn't let me touch her because of her morning sickness, which of course took me back to my abandonment issues. I didn't get hugged as a child and then my wife wouldn't hug me! Oh, did I mention she had two kids when we got married? So we were newlyweds with crazy heads and sick hearts, she was pregnant, evil, and withholding sex from me so I was sexually frustrated; I'd inherited two kids, we had money issues, and by the way, I had just been elected pastor of a church that would soon put me out. (Get my first book titled, *The Blessing Behind Closed Doors* for more details).

There is no way we should have gotten married that soon. We needed extensive counseling and small group work. Before marital counseling, we both needed to go to individual counseling. I think that's worth repeating. BEFORE MARITAL COUNSELING, WE BOTH NEEDED INDIVIDUAL COUNSELING!

DIAGNOSE IT SO YOU CAN DEAL WITH IT

If you're reading this thinking, "I don't need all that clinical, psychological babble Dr. Vernon is talking about," you're probably one of the craziest people reading this! I'm joking, but in a sense, it is crazy not to get as healthy as possible before marriage.

The best gift you can give your future spouse is a healthy you. You need to be honest with yourself about your home of origin issues. Pretty much all of us have dealt with something in life that threw us off a little, or maybe a lot. Unless you're a virgin, you have to work through who you've been to bed with and why. Were you using women because you were mad at your mom? Were you starving for affection from a man because your father wasn't present? Is there unresolved anger in you that might actually cause you to slap your future wife if she speaks to you disrespectfully when you're having a bad day? Have you had so much sex with so many people that right now no one person can satisfy your twisted sexual desires? You must look in the mirror and be honest about who you see and what's really wrong with them.

I asked my Director of Counseling, Elder Sherdene Simpson, M. Ed., P.C., M.F.T., to provide me with all the resources we demand any and every couple use before we conduct their wedding ceremony, so that I could include them here. A couple can certainly go to another venue and get married; however, we have discovered over the past ten years that couples who decide to go outside of our premarital program and get married often find their way back home to our counseling program.

Many couples share that they minimized the importance of marital preparation. They expressed that they truly underestimated the challenges of marriage and assumed that the issues (individually and with others) that they had prior to marriage would disappear. In fact, research shows that issues that are left unaddressed often times illuminate during the marriage.

We will not marry a couple who is living together and/or having premarital sex; marriage is special and sacred. If you don't learn that before marriage, you probably won't afterwards. We keep it pretty simple; if you want to get married at "THE WORD", you will do it our way. We take marriage seriously and we will not marry a couple that has not worked to get as healthy as possible before the wedding.

Full disclosure prior to marriage is important to building the foundation of your covenant. This includes mental and physical illnesses, which should not be kept a secret, especially if you know that you are currently taking medication. We have discovered in working with couples that it is impossible to hide a mental illness once you are married and living with the person daily. GO TO COUNSELING AND BE HONEST ABOUT YOUR ISSUES! You owe it to each other.

Listed below is our premarital program, the small groups we offer for singles, and a bunch of great books I recommend you read before marriage. Don't cheat yourself or your future spouse by not at least looking through what we offer and inquiring as to which programs are offered in your area.

PREMARITAL PROGRAM

BEFORE YOU SAY "I DO"

"THE WORD" CHURCH premarital training program is designed to help, support, and equip the engaged couple with the tools necessary to achieve a sanctified, covenant relationship with God. We consider it a privilege and a serious responsibility to guide you through this preparation and to uphold biblical doctrine regarding marriage. You are about to enter a lifelong covenant, which should not be taken lightly.

The premarital program also assists each couple to identify and discuss problematic issues about things that they typically would avoid discussing until they became more serious after marriage. Each couple receives professional counseling and also participates in a premarital group that is facilitated by a married couple who serve as premarital mentors.

We encourage couples to begin the premarital process at least one year prior to the tentative wedding date. Although no one expects to learn something in the premarital training process that changes their mind about the relationship, it can happen. The closer you are to the wedding date, the harder it is to address new insights in a healthy and honest way.

Materials Used:

- PREPARE/ENRICH Customized Inventory

- Before You Plan Your Wedding… Plan Your Marriage

   Authors: Dr. Greg Smiley and Erin Smiley

- The Ring Makes All The Difference (Hidden Consequences of Cohabitation and the Strong Benefits of Marriage)

   Author: Glenn T. Stanton

- Before You Say "I Do": A Marriage Preparation Manual for Couples

   Authors: H. Norman Wright and Wes Roberts

Topics:

- What is Marriage?

- Uniqueness and Acceptance in Marriage

- Love as a Basis for Marriage

- What Do You Expect from Marriage?

- A Vision Statement

- Fulfilling Needs in Marriage

- Role, Responsibilities, and Decision Making

- In-Laws or Outlaws – It's Your Choice

- Communication

- Conflict (or "Sound the Battle Cry!")

- Finances

- Sex in Marriage

- Your Spiritual Life Together

PREMARITAL PROGRAM OVERVIEW

Premarital Orientation Program

Every couple is required to attend the premarital orientation program. During the orientation program the couple is provided with an overview of the premarital program. Couples are asked to complete paperwork and to identify their tentative wedding date.

PREPARE/ENRICH Customized Inventory

This inventory is completed by all couples prior to starting the individual couple sessions. It is one of the most widely used inventories for premarital counseling and premarital education. There are also customized versions of the inventory used for marriage counseling, marriage enrichment, and dating couples considering engagement. In using this assessment, our program goal is to assist couples to identify strengths as a couple and to build new ones, improve communication, increase their ability to resolve conflict, gain a greater appreciation of their family of origin, explore their relationship growth areas, deal with financial goals and budget, discuss personal, couple and family goals, and improve your chances of a happy marriage.

Couple Counseling Sessions

The couple counseling and the premarital mentoring small groups are a requirement for every prospective couple that desires to be married at "THE WORD" CHURCH. During the couple counseling sessions you will discuss the results of your PREPARE/ENRICH Inventory. Every couple will spend at least six or more sessions debriefing the assessment and discussing relationship strengths and areas of growth. Per the assessment and session discussions, additional appointments may be scheduled. Additional topics will be discussed as needed: i.e., building a blended family. Blended families are required to schedule at least two sessions that include your children.

Premarital Mentoring Small Group

Premarital couples will have the opportunity to develop a relationship with a married couple who will serve as mentors into the first year of the marriage. Your premarital small group will take place in a group setting and include biblical instructions and tools that will assist you in building a more solid foundation. It is of utmost importance that each of you examine your hearts and your lives to identify any potential issues in understanding and applying what is being taught. In addition, each couple will receive training materials and homework will be assigned. This group runs for a minimum of twelve weeks. Premarital Small Groups are offered several times a year on Sunday mornings.

Grief Recovery

The twelve-week Grief Recovery program is highly recommended for all couples seeking to get married at "THE WORD" CHURCH. The Grief Recovery program is developed to assist men and women in dealing with their loss issues. As humans, we all experience loss issues in our lives. These unresolved issues can create issues/

problems within our covenants. This group will provide tools in equipping each person to begin to identify and work on their loss/grief issues.

Mental Status Checklist

Every couple seeking to get married at "THE WORD" CHURCH, must complete a mental status checklist. We believe that it is important that you are honest during this process and provide full disclosure, especially if you have any mental health diagnoses. This is not a rule out for getting married at the church, but it assists in detailing your premarital program. It is important that we work with the couple to provide psycho-education that will assist all parties in making an informed decision. The psycho-education component will assist you in understanding how to live with and be supportive of a person with a mental health diagnoses. This is especially essential if one or both parties are currently taking prescribed medications.

It is so important that you work to become as healthy as possible prior to getting married. At "THE WORD" CHURCH, we offer small groups that assist in bringing healing and wholeness in areas that have caused challenges and struggles in one's life. Small groups are great environments for fostering healing, spiritual growth, and support through relationships. Our small groups assist in building a connection to and fellowship with other believers who have similar life struggles. Small groups also provide a caring environment for support and encouragement in the journey in seeking recovery from life struggles.

Grief Recovery

Grief Recovery is a small group for individuals dealing with issues of grief/loss. Loss can come from a variety of lifestyle changes, death, loss of trust, loss of a relationship and other life actions in which a person may restructure their life.

Resource: *The Grief Recovery Handbook, 20th Anniversary Expanded Edition: The Action Program for Moving Beyond Death, Divorce, and Other Losses including Health, Career, and Faith*, John W. James and Russell Friedman, Grief Recovery Institute. John W. James (Author),

FOR WOMEN ONLY GROUPS

(FWO) focuses on getting women healthy and whole. FWO allows women to travel a journey of healing and restoration in a safe and confidential environment.

Accept No Substitutes (Relationship & Sex Addictions)

Are you tired of repeating the cycle of relationships? Do you find that you jump from relationship to relationship without getting healing? Do you think intimacy is the solution to healing a bad relationship? Have you ever asked yourself, "Why do I keep picking the wrong person?" ANS will provide support for women who are dealing with sex addiction and relationship issues.

Resource: *Accept No Substitutes*, Diane Roberts, Pure Desires Ministries International, Gresham, Oregon

Boundaries (Learning How to Say "No")

Are you in control of your own life? Do people take advantage of you? Do you have trouble saying no? Do you find yourself saying "yes" but you are mad inside and really afraid to say "no"? Join us and learn how to set limits and say… No! – with love.

Resource: *Boundaries: When to Say Yes, How to Say No to Take Control of Your Life*, Dr. Henry Cloud and Dr. John Townsend, Zondervan Publishing House

Boundaries in Dating (Learning How to Date as a Christian Woman)

Are you trying to live right, but don't know how to date as a Christian woman? Are you ready to learn how to set and maintain healthy boundaries that will help you grow in freedom and self control? Join us and learn how to avoid the dating pitfalls.

Resource: *Boundaries in Dating: Making Dating Work*, Dr. Henry Cloud and Dr. John Townsend, Zondervan Publishing House

Breaking the Silence (Emotional, Physical & Mental Abuse)

Are you currently or have you been a victim of emotional, physical, and/or mental abuse? Are you ready to take your life back? This group will teach you how to be empowered to break the cycle of abuse.

Resource: Materials compiled from Cleveland Center for Domestic Violence

Healing the Father Wounds (Father Hurts/Wounds)

Healing the Father Wounds is a small group for women who have suffered broken hearts and have made wrong choices because they grew up in a fatherless environment. Even if your father was physically present, he may have not been emotionally present in your life. Many have suffered the wounds of not having their father present to speak into their life. Has your broken heart led you to make wrong relationship decisions? Join us, as we begin a journey of healing.

Resource: *Healing the Father Wounds*, Kathy Rodriequez, Pure Desires Ministries International, Gresham, Oregon

Healing the Mother Wounds (Mother Hurts/Wounds)

No one has influence on the person you are today like your mother. Did you know that the relationship that you had with your mom as a child has shaped your worldview? It has also affected your relationships and your self-image. Join us if you are suffering from unmet mother needs and desire to establish healthy relationships.

Resource: *The Mom Factor*, Dr. Henry Cloud and Dr. John Townsend, Zondervan Publishing House

Safe People (Learning how to identify and move into healthy relationships)

The wounds inflicted by an "unsafe" person can go deep. Have you ever been in a relationship where you were used, abused or abandoned? Learn how to make wise choices in relationships from friendships to true commitments. Are you ready to stop repeating the same mistakes and learn how to pick safe people and select healthy friendships and relationships?

Resource: *Safe People*, Dr. Henry Cloud and Dr. John Townsend, Zondervan Publishing House

Surviving the Secret (Molestation, Incest, Physical Touch)

Have you lived with the secret of molestation, incest, or early physical touch? Surviving the Secret is a small group for women who are starting the healing process from childhood sexual abuse.

Resource: *Surviving the Secret*, Kathy Rodriequez and Pam Vredevelt, Pure Desires Ministries International, Gresham, Oregon

FOR MEN ONLY GROUPS

(FMO) focuses on getting men healthy and whole. FMO allows men to travel a journey of healing and restoration in a safe and confidential environment.

Every Man's Battle (Relationship Issues, Pornography, Internet Sex) The challenge that every man faces… The battle every man can win! It is time to break free of sexual bondage that may be hindering you from a life of true freedom. This group will assist men who are entangled in sexual immorality (pornography, internet pornography, masturbation, or chat rooms, etc.) to experience healing and deliverance.

Resources:

Every Man's Battle: Winning the War on Sexual Temptation One Victory at a Time (The Every Man Series) by Stephen Arterburn, Fred Stoeker, and Mike Yorkey.

Pure Desire, Ted Roberts, Pure Desires Ministries International, Gresham, Oregon

Rule 9: Go To Counseling
Critical Thinking Points

_____

_____

_____

_____

_____

_____

_____

_____

_____

RULE 10

DON'T TOUCH

Sex is a beautiful thing within the confines of marriage. It is one of God's greatest gifts to humankind. Fortunately for my wife and me, with each passing year we enjoy an even deeper sexual connection. God (and the treadmill!) is making her more attractive to me each year we stay married. We are experiencing a much greater level of sexual enjoyment in our forties than we did in our twenties. I'm sure my adult kids who are single and reading this are about to throw up right now, but it's my story and I'm sticking to it.

Some of you are thinking, why is he talking to singles about great sex in the don't-have-sex part of the book? I'm glad you asked! When is the last time you heard a married man whose wife had birthed five kids—six if you include the one we lost because he came prematurely—talk about how much he loves her and loves making love to her? We must discuss sex in its proper biblical context: marriage! In and of itself sex is not evil, it's not perverted, it's not wrong. The devil has thwarted our thinking because he's a copycat. He has no original ideas so he takes God's divine designs and tries to twist them. God's original intention in Genesis 2 was for a man and woman to connect in marriage, be fruitful, and multiply. Well, there is only one way to do that, right? The only people I hear bragging on great sex are the very people who should not be having it. Singles!

I think it's highly critical that I set the tone early in this rule that the best sex is married sex. If you believe in God and the Bible then you have to stop playing with this sex thing. If you're not married, sex is disgusting, damaging, dangerous, deadly, devastating, depressing, depleting, delusional, and yes, it's dumb! Whenever you do something that can destroy your body and your soul just because it makes you feel good for an hour (or a minute depending on the person you're being dumb with) sounds crazy to me.

DON'T GIVE IT AWAY

I promised myself that I was going to write a book that singles could feel—a book that you could recommend to every single you know, even those that don't go to church. For that to be a reality, I knew I had to write it real and be straight with you about the real stuff singles struggle with.

The average single reading this has had sex already. Alright, let's stop playing, most of you are sleeping with somebody right now. Maybe not everyday, or even every month, but any time is way too much. I'm under no delusions that this book is being read by virgins only. To you rare singles that have made it by His grace to your 18th birthday or older and are still pure; also to those of you whose parents loved you enough to make you read at least this portion of the book, it's because they are trying to protect what might be your most prized possession and you don't even know it—your virginity.

If you ask the average single male or female if they are proud of the fact that they lost their virginity, I think the answer would be an obvious no. Most people didn't enjoy the first time, and sadly, no longer even know the person they shared what was supposed to be one of the most important moments of their lives with.

The final rule of dating is: Don't Touch. I'm going to make every effort to convince couples who are dating to wait for their honeymoon to have any kind of sexual pleasure with each other. Even if you've had multiple sex partners, God will bless this current relationship if you do it the right way. Right before I spend the rest of my time here, I thought young singles in their teens and even preteens, along with adult singles that have had the stick-to-itiveness to wait and stay sexually clean would benefit from the following few paragraphs.

God has designed human sexuality in such a way that there is a physical sign or proof of a woman's virginity. He placed a *do not open until marriage* seal upon the woman. This seal is a woman's hymen. At the opening of the vagina of a woman who has never had intercourse, there is a membrane which is usually **not** broken except in intercourse. Of course, with the advent of products for female menstruation, the hymen is often broken before sexual intercourse. The hymen was a natural, physical signal that the woman was not to be opened until the right time.

You know the sound a bottle of Pepsi makes when you open it for the first time? I don't care how much you try to put the top back on and retighten it; it will never sound like it did the first time. once the seal has been broken, it's broken. When a woman has sex for the first time and the hymen is broken, normally she releases some blood that ends up on the penis of the man. This blood is widely believed to represent a covenant or promise that you're the first and last person I will ever sleep with, with the exception of death. Remember, sex means covenant, so whomever you sleep with you make a kind of promise to.

SOUL TIES

The Bible says in Genesis 2:24 (NRSV): **"Therefore a man leaves his father and his mother and clings to his wife, and they become one flesh."** All right, the Bible says when you sleep with your spouse you become "one flesh!"

Now look at 1 Corinthians 6:15-16 from the same version: **"Do you not know that your bodies are members of Christ? Should I therefore take the members of Christ and make them members**

of a prostitute? Never! Do you not know that whoever is united to a prostitute becomes one body with her? For it is said, "The two shall be one flesh."

Please read carefully, regardless of whether you are a virgin or a nymphomaniac! The Bible says whomever you sleep with you become "**one flesh**" with! Don't miss this! In Genesis 2:24, it says when two people get married and have sex the right way, they become "**one flesh**." OMG! This is good stuff because in 1 Corinthians 6:16, Paul is talking about sleeping with a prostitute or someone you are not married to, and the Bible still calls it "**one flesh!**" Everyone reading this who is not a virgin became "one flesh" with somebody. By doing that you formed something called an unhealthy soul tie. In his article Untangling Damaging Soul Ties, Chris Simpson defines soul ties:

> A soul tie is the joining or knitting together of the bonds of a relationship. Godly soul ties occur when like-minded believers are together in the Lord: friends, marriage partners, believers to pastors, etc. Relationships that lack 'God-centeredness' can result in ungodly soul ties between friends, parents and children, siblings, marriage partners, former romantic or sexual partners, domineering authorities, etc. An unhealthy attachment with another can bring about a psychic control that can adversely affect the life; e.g., a mother who refuses to relinquish her hold on her children (tied to her apron strings), a person who refuses to release to the Lord the memory of an old romantic flame (withdrawing into nostalgia in times of loneliness), a person who holds a grudge or a judgment against another, someone who uses spiritual forces to control others (witchcraft), etc.[1]

Have you been depressed lately? What if I told you it's not

1. Chris Simpson. "Untangling Damaging Soul Ties." New Wine Online. www.newwineonline. com/files/pdf/publications/newwineUST.pdf (accessed October 19, 2011).

even your depression but that the last person you slept with deposited some of their depression in you? By nature, you're normally a positive, upbeat person but lately you've been sad; what if that sadness came from the girl you had the one night stand with? Sex is deeper than a feeling, it's spiritual and biblical; you have to know that and protect it!

In the previously referenced article, Simpson describes several different types of soul ties, both healthy and unhealthy, but the one most relevant to this reading is "Soul Ties through Impure Sexual Activity."

He says:

> God's plan for a man and a woman is not at all like that of the world. First, He would have them come together and bond in the area of the spirit. Over time, as they get to know one another, a bonding of the mind and emotions would occur. Then, only after solemn vows of commitment in marriage, would any bonding of the body be permissible. The world has it backwards. Generally, the first thing to bond is the body through sexual indulgences of various degrees. Then, due to strong physical attraction, a couple will get married (if they even do that anymore). After awhile, they come to know one another in their soul, mind, and emotions. That's when they begin to discover that they're really not so compatible after all. The woman discovers that her attractive husband has an abusive, violent streak. The man finds that the sweet lady he married is full of insecurity and control.[2]

To all virgins reading this, know that you have something money can't buy—your innocence. On your honeymoon night you

2. Chris Simpson, Damaging Soul Ties.

have a golden opportunity to give your spouse something that every non-virgin reading this wishes they could. YOU CAN GIVE THEM YOURSELF, PURE AND UNTOUCHED! I've officiated more weddings than I can remember. To this day, I have never married two virgins. Can you imagine on your wedding day standing there with your white tuxedo on watching your beautiful, saved, sexy, fiancée walk down the aisle toward you? She's never been touched and neither have you. As you're repeating your vows, you're looking into her beautiful eyes and thinking very spiritual thoughts like, I'M GOING TO KILL THAT TONIGHT! Seriously folks, or should I say spiritually folks, virginity is a precious thing. Don't give it away!

Oh, let me answer the question you non-virgins might be asking. "What if the person they marry is no good in bed?" That's another good thing about staying a virgin until marriage. No matter how it goes the first time, IT'S THE BEST YOU'VE EVER HAD! **When physical virginity is lost, it is lost forever, but the virginity of heart can be restored-through the power of the Holy Spirit.** Even though you can't regain your physical virginity, you can repent of your sins-sexual and otherwise-and God will give you a clean heart, a new heart, a childlike heart, a virginal heart. He will take your heart of stone and exchange it for a heart of flesh. In God's eyesight, you will become a virgin again in heart. You will be just as if you had never sinned or done anything wrong.

As Paul wanted to do with the Corinthians, so I want to do with you. I want to present you as pure virgins to our Bridegroom, Jesus Christ!!!

Prayer:

Heavenly Father, I realize tonight, that through a combination of sin, self, the world, and Satan, I have lost my virginity. I have allowed other people and other things to penetrate my life and have forfeited my purity, depriving my future spouse of an untouched body and soul and sinning against You. I know that at certain points I have willfully pursued other lovers, and I acknowledge the sinfulness of my attitudes and actions. I repent of those attitudes and actions. I am sincerely sorry for the relational pain I have caused others and You.

I accept Your forgiveness right now!

I renounce any and all illegitimate suitors to my body and to my heart, and wholeheartedly reserve myself for You and the one person You have for me. I reserve myself for the moral, emotional, attitudinal, spiritual virginity, which the locusts of hell have eaten up.

Help me to walk in the newness of life that the blood of Jesus Christ provides.

DO THIS ONE RIGHT

There's a great story I'd like to end this book with.

Several years ago, a young man in our church, Antonio, who was engaged to be married to a young lady in our church, Rachael, came to my office and informed me that he had made a decision regarding their engagement. He had decided that not only would he not touch her or have sex with her before honeymoon night, but that he would not kiss her either, until they met at the altar.

I was taken aback by his announcement, and at the time, it seemed so farfetched to me that I didn't believe him, nor did I know if I agreed with him. I didn't doubt his sincerity, but I had never heard of anyone attempting to do such a thing then or since, and to make such a bold declaration seemed a bit impractical to me. Still, he was firm and sincere, so I didn't try to discourage him. I just said, "okay," and left it at that.

Every week thereafter, I asked him if he had kissed her, fully anticipating an affirmative answer, but each week, his answer would be, "No." Their wedding date grew closer, and so did my eagerness to learn if he had kept his word. As time passed, with each week, "Pastor, no, I have not kissed her," I became further absorbed in his plight.

By the time their wedding day arrived, Antonio was full of anticipation. They had made it to their big day—without touching or kissing. To add to the grandeur of an already beautiful day, Rachael and Antonio had come up with an impressive idea for their wedding that was different from any other that I had ever done. They had decided that Rachael would walk down the aisle first, and Antonio would succeed her once she reached the altar. They wanted to symbolize Christ (the Bridegroom), coming for His church (the bride), and saw a no more perfect way to emulate this than by using their ceremony as an illustration.

Rachael was a gorgeous bride, and from our location in my office, Antonio and I could see her saunter slowly down the aisle through a small opening in the door. Once she was just about at the altar, Antonio dashed out of another door and ran around the building so that he could literally follow in her footsteps and meet her at the end of the aisle, in front of the altar.

He strolled down the walkway, just as giddy and happy as any man could be. They were soon repeating their vows, and the moment came when I said the words that the two of them and many of you reading this can't wait to hear. "By the power vested in me by the state of Ohio and the authority of Jesus Christ, our Lord and Savior, I now pronounce you husband and wife. You may kiss your bride."

When Antonio lifted her veil, the anointing was so great in that moment that it took everything in me to remain standing and get through the rest of the ceremony. God's presence encased their union. I had never felt anything so pure and powerful during a wedding ceremony, and I still haven't. They did it right. They made it to their wedding day without sexually or physically overstepping any spiritual or moral boundaries, and God blessed them.

Antonio and Rachael are still happily married and in love to this day, with two beautiful boys and are now over our Singles Ministry, teaching others who are where they were just a few years ago: the blessing in doing it the right way.

Regardless of what they'd done in their past, their relationship was a virgin relationship. They were virgins in Christ. They had never experienced what it was like to be sexually intimate with one another before their wedding night, and had never felt each other's lips before I pronounced them husband and wife.

Decide now that no matter what you've done in your previous relationships or what you've done outside of or independent of your previous relationships, you will do the next one right. This may sound extreme or old-fashioned, but consider Rachael and Antonio's method. I realize this rule is "Don't Touch," but it could just as easily be, "Don't Touch, Hug, or Kiss." Abstain from it all if you can. It is very difficult to hug without kissing, to kiss without touching, and then once you start touching, it's difficult to not go further, and we all know where the road leads if you "go further."

Also, wouldn't it be wonderful to be able to tell your children that you did it God's way? Who could be a more influential example to your children than you of God's grace and favor? What if you could save your son or daughter from years of heartache and angst by simply having a story to share with them that would inspire them to want to do it God's way?

By no means am I insinuating that abstaining from all physicality is easy; it's not. As a single this close to being married, you're in a precarious place. You're with the person who you love more than anything and will ultimately spend the rest of your life with, and your desire to be with them physically has probably never been stronger. Yet, you have to stay as far away from romantic physical interaction as possible. That's tough, but Rachael and Antonio are living proof that it can be done. You too can have a virgin relationship—in Christ—irrespective of your past choices, and the Spirit of the Lord revealed to me that He will honor the discipline and sacrifice of your singlehood by blessing your marriage if you abstain. God is a God of another chance. Believe that and receive it.

Rule 10: Don't Touch
Critical Thinking Points

_____

_____

_____

_____

_____

_____

_____

_____

_____

BIBLIOGRAPHY / REFERENCES

Arterburn, Stephen, Fred Stoeker, and Mike Yorkey. Every Man's Battle: Winning the War on Sexual Temptation: One Victory at a Time. Colorado Springs: WaterBrook Press, 2000.

Chapman, Gary D. The Five Love Languages: How to Express Heartfelt Commitment to Your Mate. New ed. Northfield: Northfield, 1995.

Cloud, Henry, and John Townsend. Boundaries in Dating: Making Dating Work. Grand Rapids: Zondervan, 2000.

Boundaries: When to Say Yes, When to Say No, to Take Control of Your Life. Grand Rapids: Zondervan, 2004.

The Mom Factor. Grand Rapids: Zondervan, 1999.

Safe people: How to Find Relationships That are Good for You and Avoid Those That Aren't. Grand Rapids: Zondervan, 1995.

James, John W. The Grief Recovery Handbook: 20th Anniversary Edition. New York: HarperCollins, 2009.

Legg, Chris. "5 Greek Words for Love." Chris Legg, LPC. http://chrismlegg.com/2009/10/01/5-greek-words-for-love-agape/ (accessed October 16, 2011).

Roberts, Ted. Pure Desire: Helping People Break Free from Sexual

Struggles. Ventura: Regal Books, 1999.

Rodriguez, Kathy, and Pam Vredevelt. Surviving the Secret. New expanded ed. Grand Rapids: F.H. Revell, 1992.

Simpson, Chris. "Untangling Damaging Soul Ties." New Wine Online. www.newwineonline.com/files/pdf/publications/ newwineUST.pdf (accessed October 19, 2011).

Thomas, Gary. Devotions for a Sacred Marriage: A Year of Weekly Devotions For Couples. Grand Rapids: Zondervan, Kindle Edition, 2009.

    Sacred Marriage: What If God Designed Marriage to Make Us Holy More Than to Make Us Happy? Grand Rapids: Zondervan, Kindle Edition, 2008.

Todorova, Aleksandra. "The Six Financial Mistakes Couples Make - SmartMoney.com." Online Investing: Stocks, Personal Finance & Mutual Funds at SmartMoney.com - SmartMoney.com. Web. 7 Oct. 2011. <http://www. smartmoney.com/spend/family-money/the-six-financial-mistakes-couples-make-15414/>.

Vernon, R.A. The Blessing Behind Closed Doors. Cleveland: Victory Media and Publishing. 2007.